RAILWAYS'
STRANGEST®
TALES

Other titles in the STRANGEST series

RAILWAYS' STRANGEST® TALES

Extraordinary but true stories from almost
200 years of rail travel

TOM QUINN

PORTICO

First published in the United Kingdom in 2017 by
Portico
43 Great Ormond Street
London
WC1N 3HZ

An imprint of Pavilion Books Company Ltd

ISBN 978-1-91104-280-8

A CIP catalogue record for this book is available from the British Library.

10 9 8 7 6 5 4 3 2 1

Reproduction by Mission Productions Ltd, Hong Kong
Printed and bound by CPI Group (UK) Ltd, Croydon, CR0 4YY

This book can be ordered direct from the publisher at www.pavilionbooks.com

CONTENTS

'I consider,' said Mr Weller, 'that
the rail is unconstitootional and an
inwassion o' priwileges...'

Charles Dickens, Master Humphrey's Clock *(1840)*

STEAM TRIALS

ENGLAND, 1819

When virtually every inch of Durham and Northumberland was given over to coal mining, the problem of getting the coal out of the pits produced the idea of carriages or wagons on fixed rails long before Stephenson's *Rocket* made rail travel something that we would recognise today. The mine owners first attempted to use a steam-driven engine to drag their carts and carriages along the rails just after the turn of the eighteenth century.

Trials continued for the first decade of the new century and the new system was welcomed everywhere as a marvellous improvement. When steam power reached one particular pit, it was greeted with such excitement that the mine owners, their friends and local dignitaries gathered to watch the first load of coal hauled from beneath the ground. But, as they watched that first trainload of coal puff its way up the track, their enthusiasm quickly turned to terror – as the engine reached the assembled crowd, it erupted in a huge fireball! This was no ordinary explosion – shards of metal ricocheted in every direction, while lumps of coal sped away from the core of the blast like deadly missiles. Dozens were injured and, when the dust settled after that short fateful journey, 13 lay dead, including several of the mine owners.

MAJOR OPENING
ENGLAND, 1825

Railway opening ceremonies were always extraordinary events, but perhaps the most extraordinary of all was the opening of the Stockton and Darlington Railway in 1825. The event was considered of such importance that all the inhabitants of both Stockton and Darlington were given the day off work. A programme of the planned procession was published by the directors of the company and was widely distributed. It included details of the exact times that the train would pass certain points along the route.

The order on leaving Doncaster was as follows: first came locomotive No. 1, driven by the great George Stephenson himself, and after it six wagons loaded with coal and flour, then a covered wagon containing the directors. Next came 21 coal wagons filled up with temporary seats for passengers, and finally six more wagons loaded with coal.

A man on a horse, carrying a huge flag with the motto of the company inscribed on it, headed the procession by trotting right in front of the moving train.

The procession had enormous difficulty starting because huge crowds swarmed across the line, but once clear of this, Stephenson put his engine to the test and reached what the passengers later described as the terrifying speed of 12mph (19.3km/h). The horseman with the flag was at last overtaken and dropped out of the procession.

On the train's arrival at Darlington, the whole town was present to greet the intrepid travellers. Many people had viewed the journey as such a hazard-filled enterprise that they had confidently predicted that those on the train would not survive the journey.

But they did arrive safely and the procession was then rearranged; more wagons were added until the engine was pulling a total of 150 passengers as well as a large brass band. When the train arrived back at Doncaster, the band, passengers and railway officials formed up in procession and marched to the town hall, where a huge dinner wound up the proceedings.

In effect, this day marked the beginning of the railway, a mode of travel that, within 50 years, had spread across Europe and America and penetrated into some of the most remote corners of the world, transforming people's lives forever.

FLOATING LINE
ENGLAND, 1825

Perhaps the most extraordinary railway line ever to have existed – at least in terms of the materials used to build it – was the Durango line in Mexico. Throughout its length the ballast was made from silver ore, the sleepers from ebony. In the UK, perhaps the most remarkable line was that built by George Stephenson over Chat Moss, a huge peat bog 12 square miles (31.1sq. km) and 30ft (9.1m) deep that had to be crossed in order that the Liverpool–Manchester line could be completed.

Every engineer said that the track could not be laid across the moor – it was simply impossible. But being one of the most stubborn men who ever lived – not to mention the fact that he was absolutely convinced of his own abilities – Stephenson refused to accept that it could not be done. He decided to build a floating trackway. He put a thick layer of broom and heather on the surface of the bog and overlaid it with brushwood and wooden hurdles. Layer upon layer was added until the soggy quagmire could take no more. On this dense brushwood raft temporary sleepers were laid. The work was slow and incredibly expensive and laborious because every ounce of material had to be brought to the site in trucks pushed along the track manually.

Once the sleepers were in position on the floating raft, the spaces between them were stuffed with heather rather than ballast, and tar barrels were laid end to end along the length of the track and down at the sides of the raft to act as a drain. The most difficult part of the job was joining the floating line to the solid sections at either end of the moor. At the Manchester end, tens of thousands of tons of gravel were poured into the seemingly bottomless pit of the moor. All of it vanished, and again the experts told Stephenson it could not be done. He, however, refused to give up, and month after month, the gravel continued to be poured into the moss. At last, the gravel bank rose out of the waters and the track connection could be made. Those who travelled on that early line would hardly have realised that they were enjoying one of the world's most remarkable railway journeys on Stephenson's floating roadway.

STEPHENSON CROSS-EXAMINED

ENGLAND, 1827

Just how extraordinary the whole idea of rail travel once seemed can be judged by a remarkable exchange between the great railway pioneer George Stephenson and a parliamentary commission. Stephenson was examined by a commission that was openly hostile to the whole theory and practice of rail travel. They believed that neither men nor materials were capable of withstanding the terrible shocks and strains of high-speed travel – by high speed they meant 12mph (19km/h). So the commission was entirely bent on discovering the terrible dangers of railway travel from the man who was said to know most about it, namely George Stephenson, the father of the railway and one of the greatest engineers of the age.

One highly sceptical barrister, who was entirely ignorant of anything to do with engineering or railways, opened the questioning: 'Of course, when a body is moving upon a road, the greater the velocity the greater the momentum that is generated?'

'Certainly,' came Stephenson's reply.

'What would be the momentum of 40 tons moving at the rate of 12 miles an hour?'

'It would be very great.'

'Have you seen a railroad that would stand that?'

'Yes.'

'Where?'

'Any railroad that would bear going 4 miles an hour; I mean to say that, if it would bear the weight at 4 miles an hour, it would bear it at 12.'

'Taking it at 4 miles an hour, do you mean to say that it would not require a stronger railway to carry the same weight 12 miles an hour?'

'I will give an answer to that. Everyone, I dare say, has been over ice, when skating, or seen persons go over; and they know that it would bear them at a greater velocity than it would if they went slower; when it goes quickly, the weight in a manner ceases.'

'Is not that dependent upon the hypothesis that the railroad is perfect?'

'Yes; and I mean to make it perfect.'

Stephenson's great difficulty was to persuade someone with no knowledge of engineering that something that seemed to defy common sense could be true. To the untrained mind it seemed quite bizarre, not to say unbelievable, that something very heavy, like a train, travelling at great speed on metal tracks could stay upright. The questioning continued.

'Do not wrought-iron rails bend?' said the MP. 'Take Hetton Colliery, for instance.'

'They are wrought iron, but they are weak rails.'

'Do you not know that they bend?'

'Perhaps they may, not being made sufficiently strong.'

'And if made sufficiently strong, that will involve an additional expense?'

'It will.'

'You say the machine can go at the rate of 12 miles an hour. Suppose there is a turn upon the road, what will become of the machine?'

'It would go round the turn.'

'Would it not go straight forward?'

'No.'

'What is to be the height of the flange of the wheel?'

'One inch and a quarter.'

'Then if the rail bends to the extent of an inch and a quarter, it will go off the rail?'

'It cannot bend. I know it is so in practice.'

'Did you ever see 40 tons going at the rate of 12 miles an hour?'

'No; but I have seen the engine running from 8–10 miles round a curve.'

'What was the weight moved?'

'I think little, except the engine.'

'Do you mean to tell us that no difference is to be made between those 40 tons after the engine, and the engine itself?'

'It is scarce worth notice.'

'Then, though the engine might run round and follow the turn, do you mean to say that the weight after it would not pass off?'

'I have stated that I never saw such a weight move at that velocity; but I could see at Killingworth that the weight was following the engines, and it is a very sharp curve: it is a sharper curve there than I should ever recommend to be put on any railroad.'

'Have you known a stage-coach overturn, when making not a very sharp curve, when going very fast?'

'That is a different thing: it is top-heavy.'

'Will none of your wagons be top-heavy?'

'They will not.'

Stephenson won the day despite the commission's scepticism. And the rest, as they say, is history.

SITTING ON THE VALVE
AMERICA, 1830

The first locomotive ever built in the USA was the *Best Friend*, built by E.L. Miller of the West Point Foundry for the Charleston and Hanbury Railroad Company of South Carolina in 1830. Miller faced strong opposition to his plan to start building locomotives and couldn't raise any money from investors or banks, so he used his own money and his own initiative.

Best Friend had a vertical boiler with no fire tubes and looked pretty much like a giant beer bottle, but all those who saw it were astonished by this new and marvellous machine. At a time when most people still travelled by horse and had never seen anything mechanical that was capable of travelling at speed, *Best Friend* was an extraordinary sight – but not, alas, for long.

The fact that machines were so little understood at this time led to many mishaps and occasionally a serious accident. The fate of the *Best Friend* is a case in point. The only man who really knew how it worked and who understood its limitations was the man who built it. And his explanations to his staff about how it worked, and the intricacies of its operation, must have largely fallen on deaf ears. They viewed *Best Friend* – and the reaction was the same for very early locomotives wherever and whenever they were introduced across the world – as a kind of mechanical horse. If you mistreated a horse it might kick you or, ultimately, die – but that was about the limit of possibilities. Machines – particularly iron horses – must, they thought, be the same. But of course they weren't.

Thus it happened that an inexperienced fireman on *Best Friend* was having his lunch one fine day after a long morning's stoking when his peaceful half-hour was disturbed by the noise of steam escaping from the boiler. At first he took no notice, but then the noise began to annoy him. He put up with it for a while longer and then decided it was ruining his appetite and something had to be done. But what could he do? All he'd been trained to do was stoke the firebox. Then horse mentality entered the equation. If something is making a noise that you don't like, you shut its mouth – and that's exactly what he tried to do with *Best Friend*.

The noise was coming from the safety valve, so the fireman sat on it and happily continued eating. Some time later there was an explosion so loud that it was heard halfway across the state. *Best Friend* was reduced to a few tangled pieces of metal and very little of the fireman was ever found. Luckily, however, very few other people were around at the time of the accident, because anyone within 50 yards (45m) of the explosion would almost certainly have been killed.

SCOFFING AT A PIONEER
ENGLAND, 1830

In these days of lightning-fast express trains it is hard to realise that 150 years ago the locomotive was in its infancy and its ultimate possibilities were not dreamed of. At that time a well-known resident of Liverpool said that if it were ever proved possible for a locomotive engine to travel at 10mph (16.1km/h), he would eat a stewed engine-wheel for breakfast. Whether the gentleman lived long enough to enjoy this curious meal is not recorded.

The press almost universally scoffed at the same idea of rapid train travel, declaring it impossible and denouncing its advocates as lunatics and fanatics. 'Twelve miles an hour,' exclaimed the *Quarterly Review* in 1825. 'Twelve miles an hour! As well might a man be shot out of a Congreve Rocket.'

In about 1830, the great pioneering steam engineer George Stephenson was cross-examined (and not for the first time!) by a parliamentary committee, with regard to constructing a railroad from Liverpool to Manchester. The interview was recorded for posterity by a local newspaper reporter.

'Well, Mr Stephenson, perhaps you could go 17 miles an hour?'

'Yes,' was the reply.

'Perhaps some 20 miles might be reached?'

'Yes, certainly.'

'Twenty-five, I dare say, you do not think impossible?'

'Certainly not impossible.'

'Dangerous?'

'Certainly not.'

'Now, tell me, Mr Stephenson,' said the parliamentary member with indignation, 'will you say that you can go 30 miles?'

'Certainly,' was the answer, as before.

Questions ended for the time, and the wiseacres of the committee burst into a roar of laughter. But Stephenson built the road and, on his trial trip, astonished the world with a speed of 36mph (57.9km/h).

RAIL SURVEYORS IN THE SCHOOLYARD

ENGLAND, 1831

Once parliament had taken to the idea of railways, it took to them wholeheartedly. So much so, in fact, that it quickly passed some of the most remarkable legislation ever enacted. The legislation gave railway engineers and surveyors powers that made them seem at times above the law. Much of this allowed railway surveyors to go wherever they pleased. And if this meant climbing on someone's roof, or traipsing through their garden, or even entering the house, it was allowed under the various railways acts passed in the early part of the nineteenth century.

Landowners were outraged at any invasion of their property, and numerous instances are recorded of surveyors being attacked or shot at by irate landowners who believed – foolishly as it turns out – that the rights of property and the laws of trespass superseded the new laws governing the railways. They did not. Railways were the new thing, and they took precedence over pretty much everything. An example of what this extraordinary situation could lead to was recorded by a London reporter who heard of a case of a schoolmaster in Camden finding the peace of his family disturbed by the announcement one Saturday morning that strange men were clambering over his garden wall. On sallying forth, indignant, to demand the reason for the intrusion, he found the men coolly engaged, with hammers and cold chisels, in boring a hole through the wall of his summer-house.

As bad luck would have it, the schoolmaster's house was in the way of the proposed railway. But first there had to be a survey, and it was mandatory under the new laws that in order to complete the survey the schoolmaster's house and garden had to be invaded.

For the sake of convenience, the surveying party always carried a ladder. They used this at the schoolmaster's house to climb on to a flat roof behind his sitting room. On the day in question, the schoolmaster looked up to see a pair of legs descending from beneath a blue mackintosh. The owner of the legs and one or two assistants were carefully fixing a theodolite on the flat roof, and marking with penknives the exact spot occupied by each of the three legs of the instrument.

The outraged schoolmaster, thinking the law must be on his side, leapt out through the window on to the roof and the following conversation – meticulously recorded by one of the railwaymen's assistants – took place.

'Who are you, sir, and how dare you come on to my roof?'

'Sir, I am an assistant of Mr Robert Stephenson and I am engaged on a survey for the Euston Grove extension of the London and Birmingham Railway.'

'And what business have you on my premises?'

'The centre line of the railway passes exactly beneath the plumb-bob of my instrument.'

'Don't talk to me of plumb-bobs, sir; how dare you climb up there and to have the impertinence to stare in at my windows?'

'If you will have the kindness to look at this book . . .'

'Don't talk to me of books! I say how dare you come here.'

'That is just what I produced the book to explain, sir . . .'

'What on earth do you mean, sir?'

'I mean, sir, this is the Act of Parliament in virtue of which the officers of the company are authorised to enter on the properties scheduled in the book of reference for the purposes of the survey.'

'Hang the officers of the company! And the purposes of survey! And you too, sir! Once and for all, will you leave my premises directly?'

'I regret that my duty forbids me to do so, sir, but we will be as rapid in our work and give you as little annoyance as possible.'

'Then, sir, I shall instantly send for a policeman.'

'Perhaps that will be the most satisfactory course, sir. The policeman will no doubt convince you we are only doing our duty.'

A policeman was sent for, and the schoolmaster arrested for impeding the rapid progress of the great invention of the age.

FIRST-HAND ACCOUNT
ENGLAND, 1832

There are very few first-hand accounts of what it felt like to travel by rail at the very dawn of the railway era. But one man – a Mr Fergusson of Woodhill, Edinburgh – described the strangeness of a mode of transport that, at the time, must have felt pretty much like space travel today. In a note written just a day or so after the events described he wrote of the journey from Manchester to Liverpool:

We started with eight carriages attached to the engine with such imperceptible motion, that it was only when I found myself unable to read a milestone, or to distinguish the features of those who darted past in the opposite direction, that I was led to consult my watch for the rate of travelling; when I found, to my astonishment, that the next 5 miles were done in 15 minutes.

From the powers of the locomotive engines on the railroad, goods and passengers are conveyed from Liverpool to Manchester, a distance of 32 miles, in about two hours.

Among other regulations, a watchman is stationed permanently on the line every half mile to detect any stone or other dangerous impediment upon the rail. As he sees the carriages approaching, if there is a difficulty, he stops and extends his arm in sufficient time to enable the engineer to stop the train.

As we bowled along, a little circumstance, more ludicrous than dangerous, occasioned a small loss of time. The hook by which No. 2 carriage was attached to No. 1 suddenly gave way, and the engine, with one carriage only, shot off like lightning, leaving the others to follow as they best could. The alarm was, however, quickly given, the engine reversed its movement, and the whole affair was speedily adjusted.

An old coachman, who had been forced by the railway to abandon his calling forever, mustered up resolution one morning to take a trip by the railway, and, in spite of a very reasonable stock of indignation, soon felt his asperity giving way under the excitement of such a slapping pace, and, before he had proceeded far, exclaimed in ecstasy to the engineer: 'Come now, my lad, that's it, do boil up a bit of a gallop.'

FOLDING CHIMNEY
ENGLAND, 1832

When the first railways were opened in various parts of the world, local government officials inevitably tried to ensure that the launch of their railway service was bigger and better than anyone else's. Among the most extraordinary of all was the ceremony that surrounded the opening of the Leicester and Swannington Railway on 17 July 1832.

This took place with huge rejoicing, ringing of church bells, playing of bands and firing of cannon. However, during a trial run the cannon, fitted to an open carriage at the back of the train, accidentally aimed too low and narrowly missed the engine at the front. The engineers gathered around the engine said they thought a revolution had started.

But there were no further mishaps during the trial runs, and the great day began with George Stephenson driving his famous *Comet* engine. Behind the engine came the directors, in an open-sided carriage fitted with a tarpaulin roof. There were as yet no specially fitted seats in the carriage, so the directors brought along the chairs they sat on in the railway company boardroom. After the directors came ten coal wagons fitted with planks as seating. One wagon carried a band, and local dignitaries crammed into the others. The train measured 60 yards (54.9m) from one end to the other, and almost every inch of it was covered with flags and bunting. The cannon was carried on the last wagon and was fired as the train approached and then left each station along the route – but only after having been aimed carefully skywards!

The journey began with the chairman giving the hand signal that all was ready. Stephenson opened the regulator and the train moved forward, to deafening cheers from the crowd. The cannon fired, the band struck up 'God Save the King' and church bells all along the route began to be rang.

For years afterwards, local people remembered the extraordinary spectacle of the train moving through their towns and villages and across the open countryside. Nothing like this giant, fire-breathing, flag-bedecked monster had ever been seen before, and among the older generation – particularly the clergy – there were mutterings about the devil's work.

Only two incidents marred the journey and they illustrate perfectly how new the whole enterprise was. Halfway through the Glenfield Tunnel the chimney of the *Comet* was broken off after it hit the roof. As a result the directors in the first carriage were unrecognisable when the train appeared at the other end of the tunnel – they were completely soot-blackened. The train made an impromptu stop by the side of a brook and the directors all leapt down in their best suits and top hats and paddled about in the water for 20 minutes, desperately trying to remove the worst of the dirt.

The second accident occurred when a woman who'd knelt at the side of the track to pray for deliverance from the monster was hit by a horse that was trying to keep up with the train. The rider assumed she'd get out of the way long before he reached her, but she was praying so avidly that she did not see him until it was too late. She escaped with minor injuries, and the incident no doubt confirmed her worst fears about this new and entirely ungodly mode of transport.

The train achieved speeds approaching 20mph (32.2km/h) before reaching its destination and a street party that lasted through the night and well into the next day.

HORSE BEATS
TOM THUMB
AMERICA, 1833

About the time the English establishment was ridiculing its early railroad efforts, in America people were laughing a good deal over the race between a horse and a locomotive in which horsepower won. In those early days, Peter Cooper built the locomotive *Tom Thumb* for the Baltimore Railroad, and ran a race with a grey horse owned by two theatre managers known as Stockton and Stokes. The horse had to pull a wagon on a second, parallel track.

The story is taken up by a reporter from the local newspaper:

Away went horse and engine, the snort of the one keeping time to the puff of the other. The grey had the best of it at first, getting a quarter of a mile ahead while the engine was getting up steam. The blower whistled, the steam blew off in vapour clouds, the pace increased, the passengers shouted, the engine gained on the horse, the stick was applied to the horse, the race was neck and neck, nose to nose; then the engine passed the horse, and a great cheer hailed the victory.

But just at this moment, when the man driving the horse was about to give up, the leather band that turned the pulley that moved the blower on the locomotive engine slipped from the drum and the safety valve ceased to scream, and the engine, for want of breath, began to wheeze and pant. In vain, Mr Cooper, who was both engine driver and fireman, lacerated his hands in attempting to replace the band on the wheel; the horse gained on the machine and passed it, to his great annoyance. Although the band was quickly replaced, and steam again did its best, the horse was too far ahead to be overtaken again, and came in winner of the race.

This little engine was only meant as an experiment, but it was the first American locomotive ever made.

LEADING BY EXAMPLE
ENGLAND, 1834

Charles Fox was born in 1810. His father desperately wanted him to follow in the family tradition and become a doctor, but in 1831, his keenness for railway engineering, which was then a new profession, persuaded him to abandon medicine for a life on the railway. He left home and went to Liverpool.

Fox got a job with Fawcett, Preston & Co., before quickly moving on to work for Ericsson, who built the *Monitor* locomotive, and who was then designing one of the locomotives that competed at the celebrated Rainhill trials. On that occasion Fox drove the locomotive. She was called, appropriately enough, the *Novelty*. But for the fact that she blew a tube, she would probably have been the winner of the prize of £500, a huge amount at the time.

For a while, Fox became obsessed by locomotive driving – which, today, may seem rather odd given that we find it hard to believe that Old Etonians and other aristocrats (Fox was certainly that) are the most likely candidates for train driving. In fact, when the railways began, driving was seen as very much a gentleman's profession. Fox, the public school-educated former medical student, was then employed for a number of years on the Liverpool and Manchester Railway, a job that he adored. But this toff on the footplate was destined for higher things.

By 1834 he was a senior engineer at work on the Watford Tunnel, where he became part of one of those remarkable incidents that typify the pioneering spirit of the early railway. The tunnel was an extremely tricky enterprise from an engineering point of view, and during Fox's time as the chief supervisor of the work engineers were working in very soft ground. He was so worried about the ground that, when he was ordered to go to Birmingham to take charge of another project, he asked if the move could be delayed. His request was refused and he set off for Birmingham. A few days later he received a message that the Watford Tunnel had collapsed and eleven men had been killed. He hurried back, commissioning a special train that ran at extraordinarily high speeds, and found a scene of panic and pandemonium. Fox got the men together and said to them: 'That tunnel has to be put through, cost what it will, and therefore I want you men to volunteer.'

Not one of them would do so. 'Very well,' said Fox, 'I will do it.' And with that he got into the bucket, and was just about to be lowered down the shaft when the ganger – the leading workman – shouted, 'I will not see the master killed alone.'

The two were lowered into the shaft and together they finished the length through the dangerous ground, after which the rest of the men agreed to return to work.

Fox went on to design the roof over Euston station. He also built the iron roofs at New Street station in Birmingham, at Paddington, and at York and elsewhere. But the railway tunnel was undoubtedly his finest hour.

ROPE TRICK

ENGLAND, 1835

Railway owners were always concerned for the safety and comfort of their passengers, if for no other reason than that unhappy passengers would mean a serious dent in the company's profits. The concern for safety was not always extended to the company's paid staff, however, since they already represented a dent in the company profits. They were viewed as a necessary evil – which may explain an extraordinary experiment carried out in the mid-1830s.

The 1830s were a time when accidents were common simply because railways were in their infancy, and it was only when a particular kind of accident happened that the railway company began looking for ways to prevent it happening again. With no signalling, for example, trains tended to collide a little more often than was comfortable. One railway company decided that the best way to deal with the problem of collisions was to send their trains out with the engine well ahead and the carriages well behind.

It was 1835 when they first launched their scheme to achieve this. They attached the engine to the rest of the train by a rope nearly half a mile (0.8km) long. This meant that if there was a collision the engine driver and firemen might be injured or killed, but the rest of the train would have half a mile after the accident in which to slow down, with or without (depending on whether he'd noticed anything amiss!) the help of the guard in his brake van at the back of the train. The experiment was eventually abandoned because the rope proved more of a hindrance than anything, particularly as the train attempted to negotiate curves in the track.

TRUMPET VOLUNTARY

ENGLAND, 1835

Until relatively recently, Kirby Muxloe station in Leicestershire had the front of its platforms built up with square stones that were perforated. These were the original sleepers of the Leicester and Swannington Railway, which was surveyed by George Stephenson in the early part of the nineteenth century.

Stephenson was then engaged in the construction of the Liverpool and Manchester Railway, so he had to turn down the invitation to build this railway. In his place, his son Robert, who was only 27, got the job – the first of his many great works. The sleepers were just square blocks of stone that were placed diamond-wise at short intervals under each rail.

The line started off with only one locomotive, the *Comet*, which was built in George Stephenson's works at Newcastle and sent by sea and canal to Leicester. Passengers had not been thought of as cargo – trains were designed to carry coal.

But at last a passenger coach was commissioned and built, and a set of tickets made of brass was issued. These were sold to travellers then collected by the guard and returned to the stations that issued them on the return journey.

Some years after the service began the train was bowling along at a terrifying 16mph (25.7km/h) when, despite the efforts of the engine driver, the *Comet* collided with a farmer's trap. Horse and farmer were uninjured but the trap was apparently a write-off.

After the mishap, Mr Ashlen Bagster, who managed the line, asked George Stephenson if he could not fit the engine with some sort of trumpet to be blown by steam to warn horses, cows and farmers' traps of the impending arrival of the iron monster. Stephenson regarded this as being within the remit of a musician and not an engineer, so a musical-instrument maker in King Street, Leicester, was entrusted with the design of the steam trumpet. No doubt he tried to pitch it as melodiously as the old mail-guard's post horn, but, after numerous trials during which astonished countryfolk heard the fabulous blast of brass, the pressure of steam made him fall back on the cruder principle of a whistle.

A SHIP ON THE RAILS

ENGLAND, 1836

The huge success of the very earliest railways in the North of England meant that trains quickly spread across the country, including London. The earliest London service of all was the line from the City to Greenwich.

Crowds gathered in those early days to see the extraordinary fire-breathing monster that could pull huge loads without the assistance of horses. The new method of transport was very popular with the travelling public, or at least that part of it wealthy enough to indulge in what was seen as a luxury. But, much as people admired the technology, there were many complaints about the aesthetics of the whole enterprise. The chief complaint was that somehow the engines were rather ugly. Letters were written in great numbers to the railway company asking if they could not brighten up these dismal-looking locomotives. The real problem was that the first generation to experience railways judged them against the brightly coloured mail coaches that still dominated the national transportation system.

According to the then editor of the *Railway News*, the London and Greenwich Railway (L&GR) company took the complaints about the appearance of their engines very seriously. They studied the problem and after some time came up with a solution. Because the brick-built viaducts that carried the line into London looked rather like Roman aqueducts, a bright spark at the L&GR

suggested to Braithwaite and Milner, who made the company's engines, that they should build a locomotive in the style of a Roman galley.

The result was that, a year later, huge crowds gathered at Cornhill in the City to watch the arrival of a train pulled by a very passable imitation of an ancient ship.

When word got out, much of the route was regularly lined with spectators eager to see this extraordinary engine, which was – as its inventor had suggested – particularly impressive when viewed from the ground as it passed sedately over one or other of the company's viaducts. The only thing that spoiled the general effect was the noise and the clouds of dense smoke.

Despite its initial popularity, the idea of locomotives imitating ships did not catch on, and the London and Greenwich soon reverted to more practical-looking engines.

GUARDS ON THE ROOF
ENGLAND, 1836

The guards on branch trains had an appalling time in the earliest days of the railway. The brakes of these local trains were worked from the roof of the carriages, the guards riding outside in an unprotected seat at the end of the carriages, applying the brake when necessary by turning on a hand screw.

A journey from Wymondham to Dereham in Norfolk cured one young guard of any notion that travelling outside might be fun.

At the end of the train were two brake vans, each fitted with outside seats for the guards. The two vans had been hooked up to the train in such a way that the two outside seats faced each other over the roofs of the vans. The older, more experienced guard sat on the seat that enabled him to turn his back to the engine, while the young guard – who'd never been assigned to rooftop duties before – had the seat facing the direction in which the train would soon be travelling.

All seemed comfortable enough at first, though the iron framework of the seat was freezing. But as the train picked up speed, the dust, smoke and steam from the engine filled the young man's eyes, ears and nose. In fact, by the time the short journey was over, he was choked and soot-blackened from head to toe and almost blinded.

The smoke and steam from the engine was directed by the wind down the tops of the carriages and straight into his face. So much dirt and smoke had gone into his lungs that he could not speak or walk. He had to be carried down from his high perch, and it took two hours for him to recover sufficiently to return to his duties. The older guard later told his younger colleague that the trick was to wear a thick muffler and wrap it well round the head, and under no circumstances should he look up or attempt to see anything of the journey. This, of course, made travelling on the outside pretty pointless, since being able to see ahead and apply the brakes in time was the sole point of the outside seats.

After some years the extraordinary outside roof seat was fitted with a small box-shaped shelter, and then a small rough curtain was added to give some protection from the weather and the worst of the smoke and steam. The open van was the next advance, whereby a vehicle would have one end covered and designed for luggage and parcels, while the other end was open and fitted with a small seat for the guard, with the brake wheel close at hand.

OUT AND ABOUT
AMERICA, 1837

A newspaper report about the opening of the Cumberland Valley Railroad in America in 1837 reported that when the first train set off:

> Dogs dropped their tails between their legs and ran like frightened fiends, howling and trembling, to the far-off mountains. Men cleared ditches and hedges at a single bound as the hissing engines approached. Old men and women leaned on their staffs and gazed in visible awe as if Domesday was at hand.

But even after the astonishment and awe had abated, ignorance about the new mode of transport continued for many years. A reporter from the same American newspaper, who talked to many local people in the months and years after the railway arrived, once overheard a farm worker and his wife chatting to each other by their garden gate. It was a warm evening, quiet and with not a breath of wind.

The reporter slowed as he heard them talking about the new and startling invention, the railway engine.

At length, the old farm labourer remarked to his wife, with an air of enormous wisdom: 'It's a fine night tonight, Maggie. I shouldn't wonder if there isn't a train or two out tonight.'

BEDS ON THE TRAIN
ENGLAND, 1838

One of the biggest problems on the railway before signalling and proper fencing were established was seeing far enough ahead of the engine to apply the brakes when something had strayed on to the tracks, or when the train was in danger of running into another train or stationary wagon.

To get round the problem, one railway company sent a train out with a man sitting at the front with a telescope. The trial was deemed unsatisfactory because the lookout man was instructed never to take his eye away from the telescope – in practice, fatigue and boredom made this impossible.

Other problems with early trains centred on the coupling system between carriages. When simple chains were used, the noise of clanking was indescribable whenever the train slowed down or speeded up. Worse still, passengers were thrown about as the carriages caught up with and bashed into each other. One passenger complained that he had not paid good money to be knocked about as if he were a prize fighter.

Alarmed at the damage to its reputation, the railway company announced that it had found a solution to the problem. The company's new, highly comfortable train was given its first outing on a warm spring day. All the seats on the train had been sold after a sustained advertising campaign alerted passengers and local officials and dignitaries to what was described as a 'new era in travelling comfort'.

The journey was indeed far more comfortable than the passengers had dared to imagine – and how was this achieved? By the simple expedient of fitting a mattress (from a bed) to the gap between each carriage. Mattresses were also fitted at the front and back of the train to allow for bumps on the buffers.

History does not record how long the experiment lasted, but it certainly did wonders for the railway company's reputation in the short term.

EXCURSION TRAIN

ENGLAND, 1838

The first experience of the South West Railway in the matter of excursion trains was not a happy one. The line had been opened in May 1838, about a week before the Derby was due to be run, and, to meet the demands of those anxious to attend what at the time was seen as a national festival of incalculable importance, the company announced that they would run no fewer than eight excursion trains.

When the great day arrived, railway officials were horrified to discover that some hours before the first train was due to start, a crowd of more than 5,000 people had assembled at the departure station at Nine Elms in south London.

Trains were prepared and despatched as fast as humanly possible, but the crowd increased much faster than the railway could carry them away. The crowd was so vast that the station closed at 10 o'clock to keep them out lest it be swamped, but by this time the mob had got completely out of hand – they broke down the gates and charged the platforms!

A train that had been chartered for a private party was hijacked and its wealthy passengers summarily ejected, and the driver told in no uncertain terms that he must set off.

As soon as the train had left the station, to a huge cheer from the mob, the police were called, and the rest of the mob was scattered by horses and truncheon-wielding police officers. It was a scene of indescribable chaos – half the station fencing had been crushed, a platform branch of Smiths the newsagents looted, posters and railway timetables defaced. Railway company officials were so shaken by the day's events that they closed that station and refused to open it again for three days.

AMATEURS

ENGLAND, 1838

Until appropriate legislation was passed, individuals regularly put their own trains on the railway company tracks if they fancied themselves as train drivers.

In the early and mid-1830s a certain Dr Dionysius Lardner had become addicted to doing this. He had his own locomotive engine, but nowhere to run it. His solution was to take his partly dismantled engine to the local railway company tracks on the back of several large carts. He and his assistants would then assemble the engine, load it with coal and water and Lardner would set off down the tracks.

There was so little traffic in the 1830s that he got away with this dozens of times. Then, towards the end of the decade, Lardner came unstuck. It was a bright clear day and he set off in the usual way. He was enjoying himself enormously and had built up a good head of steam when – not realising that he was actually driving up the down line – he ran into the 8.15 express. The noise of the two engines hitting each other could be heard across the county, but by a miracle no one was killed. Three passengers were slightly injured and both Lardner's engine and the company's train were badly damaged. Lardner, a notorious eccentric, was furious with the company for having their train in the wrong place at the wrong time! Despite the damage he'd caused, Lardner could not be prosecuted. A change in the law was deemed necessary and the private use of railway lines came to an end.

CAVALIER ATTITUDE

ENGLAND, 1839

For the first 20 years that railway travel was possible accidents were frequent rather than serious. They were frequent because people treated the railway as if it were a toy or a harmless novelty; they were not always as serious as they were a hundred years later, simply because 20mph (32.2km/h) was as fast as they could go.

Locomotive engines were looked upon as a kind of fairground attraction, and it was not until the casualty list began to lengthen that the railway staff and the general public learned to treat them with respect and caution. The slogan 'Safety First' did not become the watchword for the railway for many years.

Every week there would be instances of passengers jumping off trains that were travelling at full speed – people who'd known only travel by horse and carriage simply could not imagine that travelling at 20mph rather than six or seven called for an entirely different kind of attitude.

Railway records for the 1830s are filled with entries such as the following:

Injured, jumped out after his hat. Fell off while riding on the side of a wagon. Skull broken while riding on top of a carriage and coming into collision with a bridge. Guard's head struck against a bridge when attempting to move a passenger who had improperly seated himself outside.

'Of the serious accidents reported to the Board of Trade,' writes one authority, '22 happened to persons who jumped off when the carriages were going at speed, generally after their hats, and five persons were run over when lying drunk or asleep upon the line.'

The cavalier attitude to the dangers of the railway can perhaps best be summed up in the amusing report of what could have been a fatal accident on the Great North Railway. A wealthy landowner who'd decided to take a Sunday afternoon stroll along the railway line in 1839 was hit by a locomotive and hurled down the embankment. On being picked up he simply said: 'If I've damaged the engine I'm quite happy to pay for it.'

MUSCULAR ENGINE

ENGLAND, 1839

In the 1830s, when the railway was still young and thrilling, neither the public nor the specialists were convinced that the right system – namely steam – had been hit upon. The fact that power that did not involve the horse had been discovered seems to have inspired all kinds of ideas for newfangled and often outlandish modes of transport. One reputable railwayman suggested a 'patent aerial steam carriage which is to convey passengers, goods, and despatches through the air, performing the journey between London and India in four days, and travelling at the rate of 75 to 100 miles per hour'. All kinds of substitutes for locomotives on the ground were also eagerly sought.

The Globe newspaper reported that a 'professional gentleman at Hammersmith had invented an entirely new system of railway carriage, which may be propelled without the aid of steam at an extraordinary speed, exceeding 60 miles an hour'. No details were given.

Another writer said of the Edinburgh and Glasgow Railway that it had:

The discernment to employ a Mr Davidson, a gentleman of much practical knowledge and talent, to construct for them an electro-magnetic carriage. The carriage, 16 feet long by 7 feet wide, was duly placed upon the rails, and propelled by eight powerful electro-magnets about a mile and a half along the railway, travelling at the rate of upwards of four miles an hour, a rate that might be increased by giving greater power to the batteries, and enlarging the diameter of the wheels.

This bizarre contrivance was described as a 'far more valuable source of power than that clumsy, dangerous, and costly machine the steam-engine'.

But perhaps the most extraordinary alternative to steam power was tested in 1839. The patent-office records for that year mention two gentlemen known as Taylor and Couder who registered an ingenious system by which a carriage was to be drawn along the line 'by the muscular power of the two guards who constantly accompany it'.

The carriage was described as very light and elegant in appearance, and capable of carrying seven or eight passengers at a speed of 18mph (29km/h). 'We have no doubt,' records a railway newspaper, 'that these machines will come into general use, as they will effect considerable saving to the company in time, trouble and expense of running an engine.'

When there was an attempt to test the new carriage, no two guards of sufficient muscular ability to move the thing an inch could be found, and the idea died even as it was born.

NEVER BELIEVE THE PAPERS

IRELAND, 1840

The railway engineer Charles Fox, who designed a number of stations and had been a locomotive driver in his youth, once found himself working on a railway in Ireland. The company for which he worked had fixed a day for the opening of their new railway, notwithstanding a warning given by one of the contractors involved in building the track, that he would not allow the opening to take place until he'd been paid.

Railway companies were often strapped for cash, even during the railway-building boom, and there had been too many financial collapses for suppliers ever to feel entirely happy about the companies that bought their goods and expertise.

The company ignored the contractor, invited the mayor of the city to start the train, had a battery of artillery fire a salute just before it left the station, and filled the special train with their friends, intending to take them to the other end of the railway some 20 miles (32.2km) away, where a luncheon was awaiting them.

The mayor waved his green silk flag, the band struck up, the artillery fired a salute (bringing down the whole of the station's glass roof) and the train started, only to be brought to a standstill within a few hundred yards by a man on the line waving his arms and shouting that the rock cutting had fallen in. In fact, several hundred tons of rock had been blown on to the track about a mile (1.6km) ahead by a gunpowder blast, thus effectively blocking the line and rendering it impossible for the train to proceed.

The chairman of the railway company was so furious that for a time he became completely unhinged – he called in the militia and tried to have everyone concerned with building and maintaining his railway arrested. Even his friends sitting patiently in the open carriages of the stalled train became nervous as he ranted and raved, and eventually crept away as inconspicuously as they could. Only the navvies benefited from the disaster – the railway owner thought they were too unimportant to be arrested and, since the VIPs couldn't get to their vast and luxurious lunch, the navvies ate it instead.

Late in the afternoon it was remembered that a full account of the glorious opening, the splendid 20-mile (32.2km) ride at top speed and the vastly amusing speeches had already been sent to the newspapers. There was a flurry of activity as various secretaries and other officials fired off telegrams to the newspaper in an attempt to stop the story being printed, but the answer came back: 'Too late – gone to press', the result being that a full account of the glorious journey and concluding ceremony appeared in the papers the next day in Dublin. Despite none of it having taken place.

HOLIDAY OUTING
ENGLAND, 1840

In these days when holiday travel by road, rail and air is commonplace, it is difficult to imagine a time when the idea of any kind of holiday was a new and extraordinarily exciting innovation. The first great era of holiday travel for ordinary people centred on the excursion train, and it is impossible now to imagine how momentous the prospect of such an outing must once have seemed. Some idea of the excursion's importance in the popular imagination can be gleaned from the fact that for the first ten years that excursion trains existed, their journeys were always reported at length in local and national newspapers.

The very first excursion train ran from Nottingham to Leicester on 20 July 1840. Half-fare tickets were issued for all (and this became standard practice for all excursion trains) but the demand was so enormous – 10,000 people applied for 300 tickets – that the company realised it had found a winning formula and began to run excursion trains every week.

Trains became longer and longer as the railway companies added more and more carriages to carry the seemingly endless stream of passengers. Since they were all in no hurry, it didn't matter that these vastly over-extended trains travelled at half the normal speed of a regular train on the same route.

On one unforgettable day in August 1840 an excursion train from Nottingham to Leicester carried no fewer than 2,400 passengers. A journalist from the *Leicester Mercury* described the remarkable scene:

The engines were massively overloaded and progress was slow. Then, at about 12.30, a white flag was seen at the station waving in the air. The enormous train – nearly 80 carriages in all – began to groan.

The railway company's biggest locomotive standing majestically at the head of the unbelievably long train seemed almost to brace itself for the impossible task ahead of it. There was a visible shudder as it took up the strain, leaned into the task and tried to move the impossibly huge load.

For a second, it looked as if this excursion was going nowhere. Then at last, after much clanking and blowing, the vast edifice began, inch by inch, to move. It was as if some inconceivably huge monster had come to life. The train had covered several miles before it reached its maximum speed of 10mph.

The driver and guard had been warned that the train was so heavy it might not stop in time at the other end of the journey unless they took special precautions. Special precautions in the event took the form of waiting until the lumbering giant had reached its top speed – 10mph – and then immediately beginning to apply the brakes. The tactic was successful, and at a snail's pace the longest excursion train in the history of the world pulled gently into Leicester station.

EFFICIENT COMMUNICATION

ENGLAND, 1840

One of many Victorian railway acts stipulated that there had to be an efficient means of communication between passengers and, to quote from the original draft legislation, 'the servants of the company on every passenger train running for more than 20 miles without stopping'.

The public demand for this had been increasing for several years prior to the change in the rules, and a private member's bill to enforce it had passed the Commons in 1867 but was defeated in the Lords.

All the railway companies were opposed to the change, the Great Western chairman being particularly prominent in his dissent. He considered such a thing 'quite uncalled for and likely to cause more accidents, by the stoppage of trains at unexpected places, than it could possibly prevent'.

Apart from such opposition as this, the difficulty was to find an efficient and relatively inexpensive form of communication. Innumerable plans were proposed, mechanical, electric and pneumatic, and many of them tried out, but none was found satisfactory.

For a short while there was a plan to employ a man to constantly walk up and down the length of the train peering into the carriages, but in the absence of corridor trains this was always going to be difficult. His sole responsibility in the event of a problem would be to run to the carriage nearest the engine and then speak to the driver through a tube. Another idea put forward as a serious suggestion was that two vacuum tubes should be fitted and a message headed 'Emergency: Stop the Train' would be inserted in each. One message would hurtle back to the guard's van, the other forward to the engine.

Perhaps the wackiest idea was that pulling the emergency cord would release several specially trained pigeons secured in nesting boxes on the outside of the train. The birds would fly to the engine and land in the cab, telling the driver something was amiss. The idea was tried in 1840 and was only dropped when someone pointed out that the released pigeon would not be able to keep up with the speeding train!

A more realistic trial involved running a cord along the eaves of the carriages from a wheel and bell in the rear guard's van to the whistle. Then a gong fitted to the engine and attached to a cord was tried. This was approved by the Board of Trade and generally adopted right across the railway system until the turn of the twentieth century.

LEFT BEHIND

ENGLAND, 1840

For many years after the railway became an accepted means of travel, elderly aristocrats who'd grown up in the coaching days got round the problem of hating these newfangled trains but loving arriving at their destination quickly by loading their old horse-drawn carriages onto an open freight wagon. They would then sit in the privacy of their carriages and get to London, or wherever, at top speed but in a style consistent with their sense of what was befitting to their station.

One elderly lord tried this on the London to Brighton line. All went well until the train reached the Balcombe Tunnel. Halfway through the long unlit route through the hill, the wagon on which the old man's carriage was fastened, which was the last vehicle, became disengaged from the rest of the train. The unfortunate occupant, realising he'd been left behind, shouted for help, but amid the enormous din of the tunnel he had no hope of being heard. Alone in the dark, the old man was too terrified to move, but within minutes, might have been killed by the next train.

Suddenly, he heard the noise of a train approaching and began to say his prayers – but he was lucky; the engine turned out to have been sent specifically to look for him. Lord and carriage were attached to the new engine and then carried to Brighton, where they arrived soon after the train that had left them behind. The elderly lord vowed never to travel by carriage-on-train again.

BLACKWALL DRAG

ENGLAND, 1840

When the very first passengers boarded the London and Blackwall Railway, they were about to travel on what even today must count as one of the most bizarre railways ever built.

The railway was worked not by steam engines that moved along the track pulling the carriages, but by stationary engines fixed at either end of the route. A rope was attached to the fixed engines and this was used to drag the carriages along the rail. There was one rope for the up and another for the down traffic, each rope having a total length of about 8 miles (12.9km) and a weight of 40 tons. And on this line one of the earliest electric telegraph systems was used to tell the engineer at Blackwall or Fenchurch Street when to begin to wind up or let go his rope.

On that first journey, the down train, as it left Fenchurch Street, consisted of seven carriages. The two carriages at the front went through to Blackwall; the next carriage only as far as Poplar, the next to the next station and so to the seventh carriage, which was left behind at Shadwell, the first station after leaving Fenchurch Street. As the train approached Shadwell, the guard, who had to stand on a rickety platform in front of the carriage, pulled out a pin from the coupling just in time to allow the momentum of the carriage to allow it to carry on sufficiently far to ensure that it stopped in the right place.

The same process was repeated at each subsequent station, till finally the two remaining carriages ran up the terminal incline, and were brought to a stand at the Blackwall station. On the return journey, the carriage at each station was attached to the rope at a fixed hour, and then the whole series were set in motion simultaneously, so that they arrived at Fenchurch Street at intervals proportional to the distance between the stations.

There were perpetual delays owing to the rope breaking, and the cost of repairs and renewals was huge – so much so that within a few years of its inauguration the system was abandoned.

THE COAL CARRIERS
ENGLAND, 1842

The idea of carrying coal by train once caused consternation, soul searching and heartache for dozens of railway directors. At a meeting in London, one director stood up and shouted: 'If we carry coal they'll be asking us to carry dung next!' So in the weeks that led up to the first shipment of coal being moved, one railway company issued strict instructions that the matter was to be treated with the utmost secrecy. If word got out that the railway was carrying coal, the directors believed that passengers would desert them *en masse*. This bizarre idea was undoubtedly connected to the fact that rail travel was enormously fashionable in its early days, and the fashionable traveller at that time was the rich traveller. There was little profit in carrying third-class passengers, but huge profits in carrying the wealthy. But would the wealthy travel by rail if they felt a trainload of coal had just preceded them down the track? The directors thought not. So, when that first shipment set off, each wagon was tied down with beautifully coloured tarpaulins, to give the impression that goods of a delicate and refined nature were being carried, rather than big lumps of sooty anthracite!

ANGRY ARISTOCRAT

ENGLAND, 1843

When the railways first began to spread across England the engineers who surveyed the land and marked out the route the iron road was to take made full use of the extraordinary powers parliament had only recently granted them. Never before had the establishment – particularly the most powerful segment of the establishment, the landed aristocracy – been put in a position in which their rights were seen as secondary to the rights of commercial enterprise.

But the government and business leaders knew that the railway was the future, that the railway meant increased efficiency on a scale never before dreamed of and profits to match. The country would prosper if railways were allowed to develop unhindered, which is why parliament gave the engineers the right to enter any and every piece of land deemed necessary for their work.

But, after centuries of having it pretty much their own way, the landed gentry were understandably outraged that their interests, for the first time ever, did not come first. Some landowners set their keepers on the railway engineers if they caught them on their land; some tried – unsuccessfully – to sue the railway companies. Others, realising that they could not legitimately stop the surveyors and engineers, made sure that their most savage dogs were always loose whenever they heard that the railwaymen were in the area. One or two of the richest, most powerful and most conservative took the law into their own hands.

One elderly aristocrat, who was distantly related to Queen Victoria, threatened to shoot the 'damned engine' if it crossed his land. For months he had to be restrained from attacking the engineers who laid tracks across his land and, when the first train came through, he stood at the edge of the line and fired both barrels of his shotgun at the locomotive. Amid the noise and steam of the engine itself no one noticed, but the next time the train came through the old man fired at the engine and at the first carriage, narrowly missing the passengers. He was subsequently arrested and bound over to keep the peace. For such a serious offence, anyone else would have been transported to New South Wales or, at the very least, locked away in Newgate Prison for a decade or so. But the elderly aristocrat was a relative of the Queen and prison was therefore out of the question.

Months passed after the second of the two shotgun incidents, and the railway companies assumed that the old man had got used to the change that had come about. But then an odd-looking character began to be seen regularly on the local trains. He had the general appearance of a working man, with thick homespun clothes very much the worse for wear, heavy clogs and a workman's pack. But at a time when few working men travelled by train because it was so expensive his regular trips seemed very much out of keeping with his status.

Then one day he was seen behaving very oddly just moments before the train was derailed. No one was injured, but the locomotive and carriages were badly damaged, together with a substantial stretch of the track. The derailment happened on the old aristocrat's land and, within minutes of it happening, dozens of workmen appeared, as if from nowhere, and, having assured the driver and guard that they were from the railway company, proceeded to rip up several hundred yards of track, on the grounds that it was too badly damaged now and would have to be replaced anyway. The driver and guard were too shaken to object, and by the time senior railway officers arrived on the scene both the track and the workmen who'd ripped it up had disappeared.

The old workman, with his fustian clothes, was never again seen on the train, and the cause of the derailment was never discovered – all the evidence that might have been revealed by an examination of the tracks had vanished, along with the tracks themselves. The whole incident remained a mystery, but rumours persisted in the area that the old working man had in fact been the landowner in disguise, and that somehow he'd managed to travel on the train and derail it just as it crossed his land. These suspicions were never proved, but curiously, a few months after the incident the old landowner retreated to his estates in Scotland and, as far as anyone knew, he never returned to England.

ONE MAN'S STATION
ENGLAND, 1844

As the railway gradually spread across the land in the 1830s and 1840s, the men who ran it became increasingly aware of their powers. Parliament rarely said no to the demands of these new high-powered entrepreneurs; if old buildings needed to be demolished to make way for the iron road, parliament usually rushed through the necessary legislation. Progress was the watchword and, since the railway was believed to be the future, the demands of the railwaymen had to take precedence over everything else. It is certainly true that deference to Queen Victoria was such that, when, for example, she demanded that the railway be routed well away from Windsor Castle, that is what happened. Queen Victoria could dictate to the railway, but few others would dare – with one exception.

In the 1840s, the quiet green countryside of Middlesex, some 6 miles (9.7km) from the City of London, had yet to be transformed into the endless urban sprawl we see today. When the railway first crossed this part of the countryside on its way from London to Harrow there was no need for a new station on Acton Lane, which ran northwards across thinly populated fields from the village of Chiswick. But the railway manager lived on lonely Acton Lane, and he needed to catch the train pretty regularly.

Which is why *Bradshaw's Guide* for May 1844 shows a new station open on the London and North Western Railway called Willesden. Prior to this there was no stop between London and Harrow. Willesden station, 6 miles from London, and Sudbury station were opened on the same day, together with those at Pinner and Bushey. Willesden was a small roadside station on Acton Lane, but it was fully equipped with a coal fire-heated waiting room, elaborate shelters and beautifully kept flowerbeds. Local people were baffled – why on earth build a station where so few people lived? The answer was simple: it was built entirely for the convenience of Captain Huish, the railway manager who lived nearby.

KEEP ON WORKING
ENGLAND, 1845

The Irish and Scots, mostly poor people from remote rural areas or from urban slums, built most of Britain's canal infrastructure and, of course, its railways. When everything had to be dug, cut, covered, built and demolished by hand, a huge number of hands were needed, and the strength and endurance of navvies was legendary. It was estimated towards the end of the nineteenth century that the railroads of Britain cost £1,000 (at least £200,000 in today's money) a mile just in beer for the navvies.

One of the most extraordinary stories about the railway navvy was centred on the tunnel at Bugsworth in Derbyshire, just north of Chinley, when the Midland Railway was being created back in the 1840s. The mouth of the tunnel fell in, and a small gang of navvies were entombed. A short rescue shaft was quickly sunk, but it still took a day and a night to reach the buried men. They were found lying, almost dying, exhausted for want of air, and on the floor their last candle was flickering, and in a few minutes would have gone out.

The rescue was just in time, but when the men recovered they told a strange tale of one of the most prosaic of heroic deeds. They had been startled by the fall of rock – there was absolutely no warning – and in seconds they found they were completely shut in. Their leader said that initially they were afraid but quickly realised that there was no point worrying.

Then the next man said: 'Well, we shall never get out of this alive, so we may as well go on with our work while we can.'

And that's just what they did. They had every reason to believe that they would be dead soon but, steadily and quietly, they went on digging through the rock face. They went on until the lack of air brought them to their knees exhausted.

Resigned to their fate but pleased they had completed a bit more work at the end, they then lay down and were more astonished than delighted to find themselves rescued in the nick of time. One of the nicest things about this remarkable story is that it gives the lie to the idea that navvies were always and inevitably beyond the pale.

SERMON ON THE TRAIN
ENGLAND, 1846

It is easy to forget how all early railway travel was considered highly dangerous. Not because the trains might crash, but more because speed was considered to do untold damage to the human body. There was no evidence to support this view but, at a time when much of science and medicine was still governed by guesswork, it must have seemed merely common sense to propose that since the human body could not, unaided, travel at 20mph (32.2km/h), it could not possibly continue to function normally if some means were found to propel it at that reckless speed. Thus, in the first decades of rail travel, children, the infirm, nursing mothers and the elderly would undergo medicals or visit their doctors for advice before considering a train journey.

A writer in the *Quarterly Review* compared the risk of travelling in a railway with that of travelling by rocket. And, in addition to the fear of railway travel, there were moral objections. One bishop insisted that:

Such things as railway roads and telegraphs are impossible and rank infidelity. There is nothing in the word of God about them, and if God had designed his intelligent creatures to travel at the frightful speed of 15 miles an hour by steam it would have been foretold by one of His holy prophets. These are the devices of Satan to lead immortal souls to hell.

Late in his long life, the writer and journalist J.W. Robertson Scott recalled the reactions of a group of his contemporaries to one particular train journey:

Mrs Carlyle, who was frequently described as a fearless horsewoman, recorded her experience in a train: 'I reached Liverpool after a flight (for it can be called nothing else) of 34 miles within an hour and a quarter. I was dreadfully frightened before the train started; it seemed to me certain I should faint; and the impossibility of getting the horrid thing stopt!'

Her husband described the same journey:

The whirl through the confused darkness on those steam wings, one of the strangest things I have experienced – hissing and dashing one knew not whither. Can it be that these terrible Monsters will ever come into general use?

Another passenger said:

On setting off there was a slight jolt arising from the chain catching each carriage, but once in motion we proceeded as smoothly as possible. For a minute or two the pace was gentle. The machine produced little smoke or steam. First in order was the tall chimney, then the boiler – a barrel-like vessel – then an oblong reservoir of water, then a vehicle for coals. The most remarkable moments of the journey were when trains meet. The rapidity is such that there is no recognising the face of a traveller going the other way. The noise on several occasions was like the whizzing of a rocket.

Edith Morley's mother arrived home after her journey and was visited not only by her acquaintances but by many strangers who came to beg for a first-hand account of the experience. She recalled that her baby's bottle had been entrusted to the engine-driver to be kept warm on the engine.

But still the religious objections continued. In 1846 they reached an extraordinary crescendo when a bishop travelled by train, moving from carriage to carriage in his full robes and shouting sermons at the other passengers, warning them that further train journeys would certainly lead them to hell and eternal damnation.

PLAYING TRICKS
AMERICA, 1847

In the late 1840s, John S. Dunlap was assistant superintendent, or what was then called transportation-master, on the Portland, Oregon line. His brother, George L. Dunlap, who eventually became one of the richest men in Chicago, was then a 17-year-old clerk in the ticket office. George slept in the big hall over the railway depot on sacking and lived out of a few cardboard boxes. He was famous for playing tricks on passengers, colleagues and even his boss, but he was so well liked that despite this – perhaps even because of this – he was never sacked.

Many of his worst tricks were played on the night watchman, who was nervous at the best of times but particularly so when he made his half-hourly rounds at night. As he went round each time he had to pull a wire leading to a time-clock. Each pull drove a pin in the clock, and, if one of these was missing in the morning, it cost him a fine of ten cents.

One dark night, Dunlap lay in wait for the watchman behind a train of freight wagons that had been left in a siding. Dunlap had a box of empty lemonade bottles, and when the poor old watchman came around the corner, peering about to see if anything had gone wrong, Dunlap started throwing the bottles, which fell on the depot platform with such a rattle and a crash that they scared the poor fellow almost out of his senses.

The night watchman grew heartily sick of being teased, but there was little he could do until late one night he spotted a shunting engine working alone and lit only by the light of the few fires still burning in the engine shed. He was baffled – no one should be working at this late hour, but he couldn't visit the shed again before completing the rest of his round. He shouted up to Dunlap and told him to go over and check who was working the shunting engine. Dunlap was delighted to be asked to do something – anything – in the middle of the night, since it might give him the chance for a prank or two. He set off across the tracks towards the slowly moving shunting engine while the night watchman headed in the other direction. He'd hardly gone ten paces when he heard an unearthly scream. He turned back and was in time to see Dunlap running as fast as he could away from the shunting engine.

'I saw the controls being worked, I saw them,' Dunlap hissed into the night watchman's face.

'Well, so what if you did?' said the night watchman. 'Who's working that engine, that's what I want to know. He shouldn't be there. Who was it?'

'But that's what I'm trying to tell you,' said the young man. 'The controls are working theirselves. There's no engine driver on the shunter – she's doing it on her own!'

Dunlap took several days off work after that and spent his nights too terrified to sleep. When he returned to work his appetite for pranks had vanished, but it took him some time to realise that he had been the victim of an elaborate hoax. The old night watchman had persuaded a driver friend in the engine shed to work the shunter slowly out of the shed at a given signal and then, as he saw Dunlap approach, he was to jump quietly down from the cab, leaving the shunter moving slowly along on its own.

None of this was made explicit, but the young man never played a trick again on the old night watchman.

A MILE A MINUTE

AMERICA, 1848

As late as 1841 it was stated as an astonishing fact by American newspapers that 'After leaving Boston in the morning, travellers would in 15 hours be in Albany.' And just ten years later that time had reduced by nearly half. The rate of improvement year by year was astonishing, but by far the most impressive journey of the era in the United States was made in 1848.

Mr Minot, superintendent of the Boston and Maine Railroad in its early days, was a progressive man, always on the alert for improvements that would make his line stand among the first in the country. One day in 1848 he conceived the idea of running a train at the then unheard-of speed of a mile a minute (96.6km/h), and once the thought entered his mind he enthusiastically bent every ounce of his energy towards realising it. He had a 10-ton engine built to order at the works of Hinkley and Drury in Boston, and named it the *Antelope*, in anticipation of its speed. It had single driving wheels, 6ft (1.8m) in diameter, and Mr Minot watched the progress of the *Antelope* at the works with jealous care, and declared it would either have to run a mile a minute, or go straight back to the factory.

Lawrence, a station 26 miles (41.8km) out of Boston, was chosen by the superintendent as the terminus of the trial trip. Every detail was carefully arranged in order to give the new engine a chance to break all previous records.

Nothing escaped the eagle eye of the superintendent. He was especially careful in selecting his men for the run.

'Can you put me in Lawrence in 26 minutes, Pemberton?' he asked of the best engineer on the line.

'It's as good as taking your life in your own hands, sir,' replied Pemberton.

'Not at all,' said Mr Minot. 'If you won't do it, I'll make the run myself.'

As every man on the road knew, the enterprising superintendent, besides being a natural mechanic, and as competent an engineer as ever handled an engine, was unlikely to risk a man's life on a whim.

'Will you do it, Pemberton?' he asked again, as the driver still hesitated.

'Yes, sir.'

'Good – I'll ride with you.'

Once a day had been chosen for the record-breaking speed attempt, platelayers were positioned along the track to make sure every last foot was in perfect order. Stationmasters and signalmen were warned not to permit any obstructions on the track. In the days before telegraphy and Morse code were commonplace, to run a mile a minute required the utmost planning and forethought as well as careful preparation. All trains were either taken off the rails completely or left in sidings, and a slower engine was sent on ahead first to see that all instructions were carried out.

The coming trial of the *Antelope* was talked of far and near, and the event was awaited eagerly in railroad circles. Representatives of the leading Boston papers were invited to accompany the superintendent, and, when the appointed day arrived, they, with a few other guests, were given possession of the only carriage that was to be attached to the engine to make the run. A large crowd gathered at the station and, amid cheers and vast amounts of hat-waving, the driver pulled open the throttle, while Mr Minot, who stood by his side, gave a parting salute with his hand.

Slowly the engine gathered speed, then it went thundering on faster and faster, the 6ft (1.8m) rods annihilating space at a rate previously unheard of. Boston was soon left behind, the *Antelope* plunged into the open country with the fleetness of the wind, and Mr Minot smiled with pleasure as he kept one eye on the steam-gauge and the other on the rapidly receding fence posts. Everything worked perfectly and the engine seemed to run ever more smoothly the faster it went.

The pace increased still further amid the cheers of the passengers, despite some vicious jolting over rough bits of track, which were numerous in those days when track laying had not yet been perfected. This only added to the general excitement when the passengers were nearly thrown from their seats as the train plunged around a sharp curve, or narrowly escaped jumping the track. Few of the guests had nerves steady enough to keep them from feeling a little fear for, after all, they were simply taking part in an experiment, and probably travelling faster than any human being had ever travelled before.

On they sped, now past a group of country people whose horses took fright and started off in all directions to escape the snort of the monster. Then the train dashed by a station filled with a wondering crowd whose cheers could be heard for just a split second by the passengers of the lightning express. Mr Minot never lost his confidence in being able to reach Lawrence in 26 minutes because he knew every detail of *Antelope*'s construction.

Halfway to Lawrence, Mr Minot looked at his watch.

'Fourteen minutes!' he shouted to be heard above the rush of wind and steam. 'That won't do, Pemberton; we are a minute behind!'

Shutting his lips more firmly, the driver threw the throttle wide open, and the *Antelope* leapt ever faster along the track. Not one mishap occurred; all the points were in perfect order, and the rails were checked and tested to the last inch.

At the first glimpse of the town of Lawrence, Mr Minot again looked at his watch. A smile lit up his face and his eyes had a look of exultation. As they neared the station he stood with watch in hand and, just as the engineer brought the train to a standstill, the timepiece marked 26 minutes.

A great crowd awaited the *Antelope*'s arrival, eager to know whether the much-talked-of deed had been accomplished.

'Did you make it?' cried out an excited onlooker.

'We did!' shouted an exultant Mr Minot in return.

In a moment, cheer after cheer arose for the men who had first driven a steam train at the extraordinary speed of a mile a minute.

The guests and the rest of the spectators pressed forward to shake hands with the superintendent and his driver, and to offer congratulations, while crowds flocked from far and near to look at the engine that had accomplished so wonderful a run.

Glowing accounts of the event were given in all the Boston papers, and Mr Minot received an ovation unequalled in the history of the railway.

THUNDERSTORM

AMERICA, 1848

The vast open spaces of America terrified the earliest settlers, who clung for generations to the safer counties of New England and the east. The great unexplored regions of the west were too much for a society that still looked back to the smaller, more densely populated societies from which their ancestors had come in Europe. The Wild West was a vast unknown and was therefore better avoided.

It wasn't until well into the nineteenth century that the railway companies finally began to push out into this unexplored territory. Despite attacks from landowners and the seemingly insuperable difficulties of the terrain, the railroads gradually moved out into even the most remote corners of the country. But there was a price to pay. Accidents were frequent, railway workers often disappeared into the bush never to be seen again, supplies and equipment vanished or were stolen. On one or two occasions whole groups of workers were besieged by native tribes for days on end. Occasionally they were massacred and never heard of again. But the most extraordinary disappearing act played out in the Wild West of America had nothing to do with workers, their supplies or equipment. It concerned a whole train.

A huge freight train owned by the Kansas Pacific Company was making its way across country in the 1840s when it got caught in a ferocious thunderstorm. Normally this would have been a relatively minor inconvenience, but the storm turned out to be one of the worst of the century, and at its heart was a giant waterspout with all the power of a whirlwind.

More than 16,000ft (4,878m) of track were washed away when the eye of the storm passed over a particularly remote part of the railroad. Unfortunately, the train was somewhere on that stretch of track when it happened. Whether it plunged into a canyon with a vast and very deep river at the bottom of it or simply came off the track and was quickly buried in deep sand driven by the extraordinary winds, no one knows. But 40 years later, after numerous careful searches, the last rather perfunctory attempt to locate the train was carried out. Not a trace of it could be found. To this day its whereabouts remain a mystery.

MY FIRST VISIT TO LONDON

ENGLAND, 1848

John Neeve Masters experienced train travel for the first time when he caught the 9.20am from Headcorn in Kent into London, in the days when railway carriages were still like open cattle trucks. His train was made up of six railway coaches and an engine with a chimney that was so tall it had to be hinged so it could be let down to allow the train to go through tunnels.

The carriages were fitted with hard benches – 'Oh how I longed for a cushion!' recalled Masters – fitted round the sides, but there was also a bench running down the centre. The sides of the carriages were high – so high, in fact, that passengers had to stand up to see over them. What astonished Masters initially was the pleasure the other passengers took in continually spitting on the floor of the carriage.

But then they were off. Years later Masters recalled both the dirt and the intense excitement of those first accelerating moments:

Well, off we went and the smoke from the engine nearly smothered us. Most people coughed, but some of us who had never been in a railway train before made out we were enjoying the all-enveloping smog. The terror and thrill of it was certainly something to be remembered. The engine had a longer chimney than locomotives have now and the chimney had to be let down when we passed under a bridge over the railway line, which was pretty often.

Then it came on to rain and most people had got a carriage umbrella, so up went those big umbrellas and down came the drips. I can, in imagination, feel them running down my back even now.

Masters went on to say that his heart was in his mouth for most of the journey, so dangerous and futuristic did the roaring monster seem, but from this most modern method of transport he quickly reverted to something he knew better:

Well, Father and I got to London Bridge station all right – Charing Cross station had yet to be built and we stayed at an ancient inn in Aldersgate Street. We took a horse-drawn cab and I can still hear the cabby swearing that Temple Bar – the old arch that was built over the Strand – made life almost impossible because it caused such a bottleneck, but I was sorry when it was pulled down twenty years afterwards.

BATTLE OF THE RAILWAY COMPANIES

ENGLAND, 1849

The Manchester, Sheffield and Lincolnshire Railway company (MS&LR) shared a station in Manchester with the North Western Railway company (NWR). At a time when each railway company invariably had its own stations and track this was a cause of endless trouble.

In fact, it got so bad that on numerous occasions when a group of staff from one company, bumped into a group of staff from the other company either on the platforms or around the booking hall or goods yard, they would shout abuse at each other or even begin fighting.

Fighting was rare, but individuals from each company would at the very least ignore each other if they happened to meet. Then, late in the 1840s, what had always been a bad situation suddenly became much worse. A Manchester, Sheffield and Lincolnshire train arrived at platform six early one July morning and the staff of the North Western were ready and waiting: as the passengers climbed down from the train they were arrested and taken to a large waiting room where they were held under lock and key for several hours.

The officials who'd locked the passengers up spent two hours arguing with officials from the Manchester, Sheffield and Lincolnshire company before the police were called and the passengers released. The MS&LR sued the North Western company. In court, the MS&LR lawyers claimed that the North Western Railway had carried out a continual and flagrant war against the MS&LR; they had, it was claimed, deliberately left a truck on a platform designated for use by the MS&LR; they had deliberately blocked a line used by the MS&LR; they had even, in the dead of night, employed carpenters to build wooden screens across parts of the station used by the MS&LR. Worst of all, they had bricked up the entrance to the MS&LR booking office and then claimed it was an accident!

The judge found for the plaintiff, and the NWR were ordered to pay a huge fine. In a case that is probably unique in legal history, the whole company, including its directors, was bound over to keep the peace and the company was warned that, if they interfered again with the MS&LR, their directors might find themselves in prison.

BARKING BABY

ENGLAND, 1849

For the first 30 years of their existence, the railway companies charged very high fares for pets. The feeling was that animals were a bit of a nuisance and might put off other passengers. High prices would ensure that only the absolutely determined would take Rover or Tiddles with them. And if they could afford the high prices, the idea was that pet owners were far more likely to turn up with a spotless poodle rather than a muddy hound, thus reducing the risk of complaints from other passengers.

The high-price policy seemed to be having the desired effect, but then rumours began to circulate that passengers were avoiding paying for the pets in the most ingenious ways.

An official who was employed by one company to find out what was going on reported one incident to the board:

I was aboard the down train for Nottingham, keeping my wits about me, and observing the very mixed crowd in the second class carriages. We stopped at a country station and a woman got into the carriage carrying a ponderous looking babe. It was dressed in long clothes, with its head entirely concealed in a shawl. Several times during the journey the half smothered infant made a noise very like the barking of a dog. The repetition of these unusual sounds aroused the sympathy of another passenger, an old lady, who remarked: 'What a dreadful cold that child has got to be sure.' The woman with the baby replied that the poor thing had suffered an attack of the flu which she was afraid would turn to whooping cough.

At Nottingham, the ticket collector opened the door abruptly and shouted 'Tickets please!' The suddenness of this outburst clearly surprised the slumbering object in the woman's arms and there was an angry and unmistakable bark. The astonished ticket collector reached forward and, before the woman could object, he lifted the shawl to reveal a not particularly attractive nor youthful Dachshund.

The official report does not say what happened next, but it is easy to imagine that the poor woman would have had to pay the extra fare amid hoots of laughter from the other passengers.

FUEL GATHERING

ENGLAND, 1850

News that a train was to pass through a rural area spread rapidly; the prospect of the train's arrival was so exciting that people would walk for miles to reach the tracks, and they would arrive early and wait all day if necessary to get a good place at the front and so avoid the risk of missing the great event.

A journalist waiting with a huge crowd to see a train pass in the South-West was astonished to see – when the train finally arrived – that the tender seemed to have all sorts of rubbish in it in addition to the coal. There were bits of old wooden furniture, fencing, even whole small trees. He made some enquiries but came up against a wall of silence and denial. Coal was the only fuel ever used, he was told.

The journalist was convinced by what he'd seen, so he began to travel regularly along the line. On his first few trips nothing untoward happened, but then, for no apparent reason, the train stopped in the middle of nowhere and, on looking out the window, the journalist saw the driver and the fireman leap down from the engine and run into a wood nearby. They came back with armfuls of logs, loaded them on to the train and then ran back to an old, apparently abandoned farmhouse and proceeded to help themselves to the logs piled up in the garden. They also ripped out the side of a wooden chicken house and tore up the wooden palings that ran along the drive to the house. It took them nearly an hour to load up the tender again with the various bits and pieces they'd stolen, and they did it amid howls of protest from the passengers, who shouted from the windows of the train that the delay would make them late for various appointments.

When the journalist later wrote his report the editor spiked it – he was also a shareholder in the local railway!

THE SOOT BAG MEN

ENGLAND, 1850

The early railway prided itself on the fact that its first-class service attracted the well-to-do, the successful and the more adventurous of the aristocracy. Refinements to the service were always aimed at first-class passengers and at the groups who could be assumed to enjoy travelling in some style. After all, this is where the greatest profits were to be made. And it is easy to imagine the railway owners lamenting the fact that it was necessary, merely to keep the wheels of commerce in motion, also to provide third-class coaches, or wagons, as they might better be described.

Third class made little in the way of profit for the railway company owners, but factory owners who might have a share or two in railway stock wanted cheap transport for their staff. Imagine, then, the horror of the railway directors when they heard rumours that the well-to-do were, in increasing numbers, buying third-class tickets.

One director simply could not believe that this was happening, so he spent several weeks travelling each day on one of the early up trains to London. He discovered that a significant proportion of those who, judging by their dress, should have known better were happily asleep or reading their newspapers in carriages made to carry only those lesser mortals who dug the roads or cleaned the sewers. Those behaving badly included landowners, gentleman farmers and even, God help us, the odd baronet.

In short, first class had invaded third, an event that hinted at the worst kind of revolutionary fervour and, worse still, meant a loss of funds for the railway directors and shareholders. This situation could not be allowed to continue. But a solution was hard to find – booking-office clerks could hardly be asked to refuse to issue third-class tickets to anyone who seemed able to afford first class. The director reported the situation to his fellow directors:

I discovered that there were certain persons in superior positions who were base enough to travel third class and in order to bring these offenders to a proper sense of their position and to swell the revenues of the company, I recommend that we introduce what might best be termed special inconveniences.

The lead was taken in this respect by the Manchester and Leeds Railway, the directorate of which brought in what was known as the 'soot bag system'.

Thus on a bright spring morning in 1850 one of the most extraordinary journeys in railway history began. A team of four chimney sweeps had been specially hired. Each was assigned a third-class carriage that was believed to harbour individuals who did not belong to the working classes.

The decision about which carriages needed 'special inconveniences' was based on observations made by a senior porter who watched to see if anyone well turned out entered a third-class carriage. He then kept a note and reported his findings to the sweeps. As soon as the train set off on its journey the sweeps moved into action. They entered the third-class carriages and immediately unfolded several of their recently used sacks and began to shake them out, covering everyone in the carriage with a layer of grime and dirt. The working men, of course, took little or no notice, since their work obliged them to wear rough and dirty clothes anyway. But the well-dressed were outraged.

What could they do, though? If they complained to the management they would be told to travel first class, since third-class passengers were used to dust and dirt and the railway company could do nothing about it.

The ruse worked, the numbers of passengers travelling first class rose, and as time passed, fewer of the middle classes risked a confrontation with the soot bag men.

According to an early edition of *The Railway Times*, other rail companies found it more convenient to make sure that sheep or even pigs travelled regularly in their third-class carriages!

SMOKING SIGNS
ENGLAND, 1851

It is difficult now to believe it, but in Victorian times male
travellers didn't like travelling with the fairer sex. This had
a great deal to do with the fact that relations between the
sexes were far more formal then than now. One book of
travel etiquette published in the 1840s recommends that
gentlemen entering a carriage where a lady is already seated
should first bow to her and then ask permission to take a
seat in the same compartment. The book goes on to explain
that under no circumstances should a gentleman take snuff
or smoke in the presence of a lady. Newspaper reading was,
however, acceptable, although novels might cause offence if
they were in French, since anything French was considered
to be, almost by definition, notoriously scandalous.

The situation became so bad on some routes out of
London that an enterprising printer began a profitable
sideline selling smoking signs. These were advertised
discreetly through gentlemen's clubs and sold to men
who had in the past had to endure a journey with a female.
The signs were hugely popular, but once you had your
sign it was still essential to arrive at the station in time to
get a compartment alone or with a fellow male. Once in a
compartment with no women, the trick was to stick one
of the carefully faked – but authentic-looking – smoking
signs on the window facing the platform and on the window
facing the corridor.

If the rules for men were onerous, they were even worse for female travellers. A woman on her own would not enter a compartment where a single man was seated, although it was acceptable if he was accompanied by his wife or a child. However, no single woman with any pretensions to good breeding would dream of entering a smoking compartment with one or more males.

It was only when railway staff began to notice that on some journeys virtually every compartment was designated a smoking compartment that officials realised something was amiss. More careful records were kept and ticket collectors were instructed to check the actual number of smoking compartments compared with the official list. No one was ever arrested for the scam – the ticket collectors were simply instructed discreetly to remove illegal signs. Among the smoking classes this was seen as a black day indeed.

SEEING THE DEVIL

ENGLAND, 1851

It is difficult today to appreciate quite how terrifying the first sight of a locomotive engine must have been, particularly for people in remote rural districts who had nothing in their own past lives to help them comprehend this extraordinary apparition. In the early nineteenth century the world was governed entirely by the pace set by the horse, and the idea that a mechanical contraption with no horse could travel at twice the speed of the fastest horse, and for hours on end, must have seemed not just fanciful but downright impossible.

There are numerous accounts in diaries of country people who, after reading about the coming of the railway in their newspapers, regarded the idea as a joke made up by journalists to fool the more credulous. There are also accounts of people seeing their first train and simply fainting or running away. A vicar took his eight-year-old son to see the very first train pass through Devon and the boy screamed and ran away and apparently had nightmares for weeks afterwards.

Perhaps the most amusing story of shock at the arrival of the iron railroad comes from a Midlands writer who recorded the words of an old lady from a village in the hills who came down to visit some relatives in a town on the newly opened North Midland Railway. On her first day wandering about the town she saw her first train.

Rushing into her relatives' house, almost beside herself with panic, she screamed:

Oh Bessie! What dusta think awve sane? Awve sane t'divil his-self. 'is yed wor all ablaze and smokin and he rushed along over faelds and 'edges and jumpin ditches and then ey sqealed loike a pig oinly 'arder. I nivir want to see im no more!

SABBATH TRAINS
SCOTLAND, 1851

The first trains to run through Scotland in the middle decades of the nineteenth century caused outrage among the more religious inhabitants who, in some cases, knelt by the side of the tracks to pray for deliverance from the fire-breathing monster sent by the devil to corrupt the Sabbath.

An Englishman arriving at Edinburgh station in the 1850s was collared by a Presbyterian as he alighted on the platform. With gimlet eye, the zealot harangued the poor traveller with the following words:

> And if we are entitled to employ our servants for railway work on the Sabbath why am not I and others entitled to reap our crops, or plough our fields on that day, or why may not a manufacturer also employ his work-people or any other work whatever be carried on? Is there any exemption for railway work or have they any privilege above any other system of labour? If once Sabbath work on the railway commences, the system will rapidly spread to every other occupation and then we are doomed, doomed...

The traveller disengaged himself and vowed to keep his Scottish travels to the minimum.

TRAIN UNDER ARREST

ENGLAND, 1852

On its own land, a railway company is a very powerful organisation, which is why railway police exist. Trespassers on railway property, passengers travelling without a ticket, individuals interfering with railway property – all are liable to be arrested and dealt with severely by the courts. For the railway was and is an important institution. But the most extraordinary arrest ever made in conjunction with the railway occurred in 1852.

It stemmed from a disagreement between the Great Northern Railway and the Midland Railway. The Great Northern claimed the right to run its own engines and trains into the Midland station at Nottingham. But the claim, and the right it bestowed, had never been tested, and few thought it ever would be. That is, until the Great Northern decided it would act on the basis of its claimed rights.

On 1 August it attempted to run one of its trains into the station, but the Midland Railway company was prepared, and the trespassing train – if indeed it was trespassing – was arrested. Midland engines appeared as if from nowhere as the Great Northern train approached the station. One got behind the interloper, the other in front. The Great Northern train was effectively boxed in and had to do as it was told. The Great Northern driver made a gallant attempt to power his way out of the situation, despite the two foreign locomotives. But one engine is never a match for two, and the train was carried off to a Midland engine shed once the passengers had been allowed to get off. And there in the shed it was left under lock and key. Just to be sure there was absolutely no chance of rescue, the rails leading to the shed were then pulled up, and there the train remained a prisoner until peace was concluded between the two railway companies almost a year later.

WIDOW TO THE RESCUE
AMERICA, 1854

The Western Division of the Virginia Railroad Company ran through a very mountainous part of the state and stations were few and far between. About 3 miles (4.8km) from one of these stations, the track ran through a deep gorge of the Blue Ridge. At the centre of the gorge – a place about as remote as it possibly could be – there was a tiny cabin surrounded by a few acres of fruit trees. The cabin was inhabited by a widow called Graff and her three young daughters.

In the summer, the three daughters walked together each day to the nearest station carrying baskets of berries, which they sold to passengers weary of packed lunches and stale beer and tea. The money they earned was a useful supplement to a pitifully small farm income.

The regular conductor on the once-a-day train knew the girls well, and when they'd sold their fruit at the station he often invited them to jump aboard and then signalled the driver to make an unauthorised stop where the track passed the children's farmstead. The children always offered to pay the conductor for his kindness by giving him any remaining baskets of fruit. He would always accept but insisted on paying.

Then came the worst winter in living memory. The year 1854 saw snow more than 3ft (0.9m) deep right across the state, and in some places where drifts had built up, it was

20 or 30ft (6.1–9.1m) deep. Then, in mid-December of that year, the weather suddenly turned warm, causing the snow to melt rapidly. This was combined with a series of terrible storms, so that the valleys were filled with raging water, from hilltops swept by ferocious winds.

On 26 December the Western Division train was making its way through the Blue Ridge with its friendly conductor aboard. Despite the pitch black, the howling wind and the torrential rain, the guard was not worried because the track had been built along a bed of solid rock, and it was impossible that somewhere up ahead it might have been swept away. As he walked through his train the guard tried to reassure the obviously worried passengers that they were in no danger, despite the fact that the train was visibly rocking under the onslaught of the elements.

Then, just before midnight, there was a piercing shriek from the driver's whistle. The conductor and his guards applied the brakes immediately and the train quickly came to a halt. When the conductor ran to the front of the train and stood by the driver, an extraordinary sight met his eyes. Out in front of the train, for 20 or 30ft (6.1–9.1m) and more, a huge pile of logs was blazing. What on earth was going on? Driver and conductor jumped down and walked the length of the fire. Beyond it, just a hundred feet or so, the track vanished into an abyss.

The combination of huge snowdrifts followed by torrential rain and flooding had torn the whole side of the mountain out. The widow Graff and her daughters had seen the huge slide of earth and rock and realised what would happen if they did not act. They knew the train was due in a few hours, so they spent that time going back and forth to their stockpile of brushwood and logs, building the fire that had saved the train and its occupants from certain destruction.

Despite the tempest, all the passengers climbed down to see the huge fire that had saved their lives. They were so grateful that they made a collection for the widow that amounted to nearly $500 – a large sum in the mid-nineteenth century. At first the widow wouldn't take the money, but she was eventually persuaded, and used it to send her daughters to school, something that would have been impossible otherwise.

The railway company was so grateful that they built the widow and her daughters a new house, and gave the whole family lifetime free passes to travel whenever and wherever they liked on the railroad.

LOST IN THE SNOW
AMERICA, 1855

In the days of old, when whole trains would scarcely weigh as much as one engine does now, a big snowstorm was the greatest dread of railroad men in the United States. A bad snowstorm would almost certainly mean being stuck in the country, miles away from any house, for two or three days at least. In many cases it was much worse and trains might be stuck for a week or more.

The winter of 1855 was worse than any in living memory. Huge swathes of the country vanished under a deep blanket of snow and the blizzards seemed unending. At Aurora, Illinois, a certain well-known character, Colonel W.S. Johnson, narrowly escaped death from hypothermia, after getting stuck on a train journey in huge drifts. Six men lost their lives in that particular storm, within a few miles of the spot where Colonel Johnson had such a narrow escape.

For 16 days, trains without number were buried under the mountains of snow that blanketed the prairie. It then took weeks to dig them all out, but, when the thaw came, two further freight trains that had been entirely forgotten simply appeared as if from nowhere as the snows began to melt. The railroad companies had been thrown into such turmoil by the loss of so many trains and by the general chaos that they'd managed to forget two whole trains!

SOMETHING TO COMPLAIN ABOUT

ENGLAND, 1856

The tradition of grumbling about the quality of the railway service is as old as the railway service itself. In many cases, some would say most, any amount of grumbling is justified, given that the standards the railway owners aspire to are rarely met in practice. But one or two individuals in every generation have taken grumbling to absurd lengths. Indeed, grumbling about train journeys has, for one or two poor souls, virtually become the sole purpose of life. Take, for example, the elderly woman who every day for years berated the poor guard on the 8.50 from London to Cambridge. Despite his patience and professionalism, her constant complaints eventually got the better of him. She had treated him to ten minutes of solid invective during which she attacked just about every employee of the railway, its directors and shareholders. More to relieve his frustration than anything he eventually said: 'I will make sure I pass your comments on when I take the chair at the next directors' meeting.'

But a season ticket holder at Chesham in Buckinghamshire in 1856 probably holds the record for grumpiest rail traveller, for this was the year in which he began to travel each day armed with hundreds of brochures and cartoons. He had complained by letter about the railway to local and national newspapers and, despite the fact that some of his letters had been published, he was still not happy – presumably because he did not perceive any improvement in the service, despite his most strenuous efforts. He therefore went to a printer with a mass of vituperative cartoons, skits and libellous satires on the railway company with which he travelled. Having paid to have 5,000 copies printed of each cartoon and skit, he took bundles of them with him each time he travelled. The idea, one supposes, was to shame the company into new methods of conduct, but whatever his hopes, his actions were unambiguous. He took a seat at the front of the train each day and, as the engine slowed at each station, he would throw out liberal handfuls of his publicity material to the waiting passengers.

A typical cartoon showed the company's train being beaten in a race by a donkey and cart; others showed the directors as slumbering dolts. No doubt the directors could have banned their belligerent passenger from travelling on any of their trains. They might even have been able successfully to sue him, but, to their credit, they put up with his campaigns for many months and it was only the danger to other passengers that compelled them finally to act.

It seems that the irate passenger had very real talent as a cartoonist and satirist, which meant that passengers began eagerly to look forward to the shower of paper that came flying out of the windows of the early morning train. In fact, they enjoyed them so much that there was a scramble each morning that could have led to someone being pushed under a train. It was pointed out to the angry traveller that his paper showers might lead to the injury or death of another passenger and that this, in turn, might lead to a prosecution for manslaughter. After that the complaints continued, but the paper satires ceased to flutter above the early morning platform.

DOGS ON BOARD

ENGLAND, 1857

The eccentric Earl of Bridgwater never married. He rarely left his estate and, as he grew older, he became ever more slovenly and bizarre in his habits. He made a servant follow him constantly, carrying a large box of snuff; he insisted on wearing a different pair of shoes for every day of the year and he never threw anything away. As a result, his large London house groaned under the weight of old boxes and trunks, umbrellas, chests filled with old curtains, suits and rugs, discarded wrapping papers, broken-down chairs and piles of assorted domestic refuse.

But among all his eccentricities there was one that distinguished Bridgwater from every other eccentric aristocrat in the land: his love for his dogs. He owned about 15 and he treated them as if they were his children. Some were strays he'd taken a fancy to while walking the streets; others were purebred hounds and gundogs, still others were tiny lapdogs. All were allowed to sleep with the earl and to eat with him.

Indeed, every day the earl would have his huge dining room laid with the best linen and silver cutlery and each of the dogs would sit in a chair in its allotted place. The dogs were expected to dress for dinner and the only time the earl shouted at them was if they happened to misbehave during the meal.

Several times a year the earl travelled by train from London to his home in the country. Normally one or two dogs would accompany him, but on one extraordinary occasion all 15 dogs set out for the London terminus. The earl paid for 15 first-class tickets for the dogs and took over two whole compartments. To make sure no stranger tried to enter one of the two compartments – this was in the days when compartments could not be reserved – he sent his servants on ahead to the station to bar the entrances to the carriages in advance of the earl and his party of dogs arriving at the station.

During the journey each dog took a seat in one or other of the compartments, and the earl wandered between the two making sure his favourites were enjoying themselves. Other passengers looking for a vacant seat found the blinds of the compartments drawn and the earl's own reserved signs posted on the windows.

On this never-to-be-forgotten journey, the earl fell asleep and, on waking, went to check on the dogs. He found to his horror that six dogs – 'I'd never met them before,' he declared later – had somehow joined his favourites. Unused to strange dogs, the earl's normally well-behaved hounds had gone almost berserk – they were barking and jumping and even biting each other.

It took the earl and his servants some time to restore order and to reject the interlopers. He was so outraged by what he described as a serious violation that he threatened the railway company with legal action, and it was only a personal visit from one of the directors that smoothed the troubled waters. Though the railway company officials privately agreed that the earl was a damned nuisance, he was a good customer with powerful friends – so the doggy train journeys continued but, so far as history records attest, without further mishap.

DUNG ROAMIN'
SCOTLAND, 1860

Mr Lubbock, an amateur engineer from Dudley in the West Midlands, was travelling on the North of Scotland Railway. The train had stopped at a station but, despite a great deal of huffing and puffing, the engine, having stopped, refused to get started again.

Mr Lubbock was irritated as he had an appointment two stops further on and hated being late. He went up to the engine and spoke to the driver and the fireman. They explained that they couldn't move because certain tubes in the engine were leaking, but help – they insisted – would be with them soon. Mr Lubbock assumed this meant the arrival by some other means of a spare part or two, so he was astonished to see a farmer approaching across the fields with a bucket, which turned out to be filled with horse manure.

There was a practice – described as almost universal in the early days of steam – of putting oatmeal or bran or, if these could not be found, horse dung into the boiler in order to stop the leaking of the tubes.

Mr Lubbock watched as the horse dung disappeared into the boiler and then got back into his compartment. Within minutes the train pulled out of the station as if nothing was amiss.

THE MAN WHO WASN'T THERE

ENGLAND, 1860

Victorian carriages were dark, dingy and sometimes forbidding. Lit only by oil lamps, they permitted an occasional robbery of a sleeping passenger, and on at least one occasion the dim glow of oil allowed a night-train passenger to vanish. It was always assumed he was murdered but no body was ever found. He'd been travelling on a train lit by oil lamps enclosed in heavy glass containers, about 9in (22.9cm) in diameter, hung through holes in the carriage roofs. These lamps were dropped into their places by a man who got on to the roof by climbing the steps at the end of the carriages. The glass lamps, wheeled along the platform in a bogey truck, which had frames for them to rest in, were thrown up to the man on the carriage roofs, who caught them with a bit of cotton waste in one hand in order to prevent their slipping. After him came a man who walked along the roofs to light the lamps.

The lamps are relevant to the mystery of the man who disappeared, as we will see. This man began his journey innocently enough, although it was later said that he was carrying a suitcase that had been chained to his wrist. When the train entered a long tunnel on the Brighton line, our mysterious passenger was asleep; when it came out the other end of the tunnel, he had gone. His friends waiting at the station were mystified by his non-arrival. Passers-by later reported that these so-called friends had been a shabby, strange and foreign-looking bunch who dispersed without a word after it became clear that the man for whom they had waited was not going to appear.

But, whatever the truth about these suspicious characters was, it is certainly true that they did not go aboard the train and check each carriage, nor did they report the disappearance of their friend to the police. Instead they melted into the night and were never heard of again. Meanwhile, routine cleaning of the carriages discovered the mysterious passenger's hat and leather overnight bag as well as his ticket. There were also traces of a sticky tar-like substance on the open window of the carriage, and one of the overhead oil lamps had been dislodged and smashed. Below it a light dusting of white powder, later found to contain traces of arsenic, had settled on the carriage seat and floor. But there were no footprints in the dust.

The London terminus where the oil lamps had been tended at the beginning of the journey employed a number of railwaymen to do the work. On the day following the disappearance of the passenger, one of these workers also vanished. What happened to 'the man who wasn't there', and indeed to the lamp man, remains a mystery to this day.

MAD WINDHAM
ENGLAND, 1861

Anyone travelling on the Eastern Counties Railway in the early 1860s might have been surprised to come across a railwayman with a difference. For on different days this absurdly well-spoken railwayman with an aristocratic demeanour and rather haughty air would appear as a porter, a driver or a fireman. What was even more remarkable about him was that he worked for no pay. The railwayman in question was William Frederick Windham, or Mad Windham as he became known.

Windham was born in 1840, the heir to ancient Felbrigg Hall in Norfolk and all its estates. He was worth a fortune, but by the end of his short life he'd squandered or given all of it away. He once said that the only time he was truly happy was when he was on the footplate of a locomotive engine, which is why he tried every means in his power to get on to the trains that plied their trade across East Anglia.

The extent of his railway work came to light when, soon after inheriting his estates, Windham was taken to court by his family. The family wanted him declared insane for marrying a prostitute, for rushing about the country throwing money away and for impersonating a railwayman. What they really wanted was for the court to agree that anyone rich enough not to have to work on the railway must be mad to want to do it.

According to the evidence given at Windham's trial, his manners and conduct were uncouth, his mental powers well below the average and his wilfulness both extreme and bizarre.

Certainly Windham had hated his upbringing, with its emphasis on the traditional sports and pastimes of the aristocracy. Hunting and shooting held no interest for him and all his talk was of railways. But kept from the things he really wanted to do, Windham grew ever more eccentric. Wherever he happened to be, and however embarrassing the circumstances, he might suddenly shout with unmeaning laughter, or imitate cats fighting, or burst into tears, or get pitifully drunk. 'Take away this disagreeable boy,' the indignant mothers of young girls would exclaim when he was taken, as a child, to other people's houses.

By preference, he sought his amusements elsewhere. As he grew towards manhood, his tutors found it difficult to restrain him from doing pretty much as he wished; and the last of them, a Mr Peatfield, who was appointed in June 1860, seems to have had little control over him at any time. This was about the time Windham began to bribe and cajole engine drivers into letting him drive their trains, an accomplishment of which he was extremely proud. But he was equally happy when acting as guard, ticket collector, sorter of parcels or porter. He obtained a guard's uniform, with belt, pouch and whistle; and in this guise he became a familiar figure on the Eastern Counties Railway. Railway officials indulged his whims to an almost incredible extent. On one occasion – unquestionably the railway journey he enjoyed most – he was driver in the morning, guard in the afternoon and porter in the evening. It was 1861. This remarkable day was only marred when, by blowing his whistle at the wrong moment, he nearly caused a serious accident on the Suffolk line.

When in London, he used to haunt the Haymarket, at that time the centre of the city's nightlife. He frequented

London's brothels and was much in the company of prostitutes but, on the whole, he seems to have found greater enjoyment in pretending to be a policeman in town and a railwayman while in the country. Although they did not provide him with a uniform, the police showed him the same kindly indulgence as the railway officials had done. They looked on tolerantly when he went up to groups of people in the street and ordered them, in the voice and manner of a policeman, to move on.

He used to threaten women that he would have them locked up – he said there were too many women in the Haymarket, and that he would not stand it any longer. The women would shout back, 'Go away, you fool; you're not right in your head!'

By the time he'd come into his inheritance, he'd met and married Agnes Willoughby, allegedly a prostitute. She was said to belong to the same circle as famous mistresses of the aristocracy and royalty, women such as Catherine Walters – alias Skittles – who appears in many Victorian memoirs.

Once they were married, Agnes managed to persuade Windham to sign all his money and property over to her. But, despite this and his passion for the railways, the courts refused to declare him insane. The biggest problem was that Windham seemed to the courts no madder than many family members brought to testify against him. But once the court had made its decision and he was released Windham headed for the brothels of London and the railways of East Anglia with a vengeance. Having been thrown out of Felbrigg Hall by Agnes, he rented a room in a coaching inn in Norwich, where he spent his days permanently dressed as a railway guard and staring out of his bedroom window, from which position he would shout and make faces at the ostlers. At last in February 1866 he died after a massive bout of drinking, still in his railway guard's uniform.

IMPERSONATING A COW
FRANCE, 1862

Excursion trains were by no means an exclusively English phenomenon. The French took to the idea with a passion in the 1860s – so much so that on the Paris–Le Havre line they often ran short of proper carriages. In any other country the railway company would have bought extra carriages, or borrowed some from another train company. Not the French. Without worrying about how the excursion passengers would feel about it, they simply added open cattle trucks to any over-booked excursion train. These were fitted with the crudest of seats in the form of rough planks laid across wooden blocks.

On one cattle truck excursion the passengers at first accepted the situation with good humour, but, when a ticket inspector entered one of the trucks to check that everyone had paid, some strange collective lunacy took hold of the passengers and they answered every question posed by the official with a loud collective 'Moo!'

The joke did not end there either, for soon it had extended to all the other cattle trucks and, unable to get anything other than animal noises out of any of the passengers, the inspector could do nothing but beat a hasty retreat. At the next station the stationmaster tried to restore some order to the proceedings by donning his very best top hat and addressing the train from the top of an apple box. After two sentences his words were drowned out by a chorus of moos.

According to the reports that appeared the next day in a local newspaper, the situation grew even worse when the train reached its destination. The passengers in the cattle trucks rushed the barrier *en masse*, knocking inspectors, porters and other staff out of their way.

When the stationmaster managed to grab one of the passengers, the others turned on him and – still pretending to be cows – ran at him with their heads down. After he'd been butted in the stomach by the sixth or seventh cow-imitating passenger, he released the man he'd grabbed and ran for the safety of his ticket office. At that point, and for reasons that have never been explained, the crowd as one suddenly stopped their bovine antics, quietly handed over their tickets and filed out of the station.

DARING FEAT
AMERICA, 1862

The train consisted of a luggage van or baggage car and two passenger coaches, with the engine *General Stark*, which had just been delivered from the Massachusetts-based Lawrence Locomotive Works. The driver was Dick Allen, who later achieved fame as Richard Norton Allen, the wealthy Cleveland inventor and businessman.

About 5 miles (8km) from Bennington, Vermont, the train hit a cow and the engine and two carriages were thrown off the track. Driver and conductor were uninjured, so they picked themselves up, sat on the track and discussed what they should do. The only way to get another engine was to run a hand-car – one of those absurd little rail carts with a rocking handle you see in Westerns – or walk. Neither prospect appealed, so they thought again.

'It's nearly all downhill to Bennington,' said the driver. 'So let's uncouple the last carriage and run it back on its own to the station.'

Today, anything like this would lead to an inquiry and the instigators would almost certainly be sacked. But in the early days – particularly with its huge distances between towns – quick expedients and great risks were often necessary.

After the passengers had been persuaded to exit the last carriage, the guard, a brakeman and the conductor uncoupled it. With a gentle push it began to pick up speed on the steep incline. The three men leapt aboard as it began to move.

At first everything went smoothly, and the conductor later described the strange sensation of speed with no noise – or at least no noise other than the whistling of the wind. But the three men were anything but relaxed – what on earth would they do, they wondered, if they should reach an uphill stretch of track?

As it turned out, Fortune was with them, and the momentum they'd gained took them over each and every rising stretch of track and on to yet another downhill section. The one exception – a stretch too steep and in danger of stopping them dead – was overcome when two of the three men jumped down and added their pushing power to the carriage's impetus. The effort proved effective and the carriage inched over the top of the rise to begin its descent once again. A wandering cow posed the next threat, but with shouts and gesticulations they managed to frighten it off the track ahead, and, soon afterwards, the carriage rolled into the station with the brakeman furiously turning his handle to slow it down.

With a relief engine they started back to the scene of the accident, pulled the other engine back on to the track and went on to Rutland at terrific speed. The *General Stark*, despite coming off the rails, was undamaged, and they made it to their destination only an hour or so late. It was a train rescue long remembered and talked about in the annals of American railway history.

PULLING THE CORD

ENGLAND, 1862

The emergency services are plagued with trivial telephone calls. The elderly will, we are told, regularly call for an ambulance if they find it too difficult to carry their shopping up the stairs; young women have been known to telephone for help if a long and delicately painted fingernail happens to snap off. But it was ever thus. In the early days of railway travel it was difficult – particularly for those passengers who'd known the coaching days – to understand that stopping a train was not the same as stopping a carriage and four.

Instances are recorded of passengers pulling the communication cord because they'd been sleeping and, having woken with a start, feared they might have missed their station. There are records of passengers stopping the train at the point where it passed closest to their homes rather than wait until it had gone another three miles (4.8km) and stopped at the station. There are even records of passengers stopping the train simply because they were fed up with the journey, and several instances are recorded of passengers stopping the train to ask that their footwarmers be reheated. But the prize for the most absurd reason given for stopping a train has to go to an old lady who pulled the communication cord on a non-stop London to Glasgow express. She didn't just pull it – she yanked on it violently and repeatedly and to such an extent that guard, ticket collector and dining-room attendant came running. The train screeched to a halt even while they ran through the corridors. But when they got to the old lady's compartment they found nothing amiss – other than an extremely agitated pensioner. What on earth was the matter? The woman waved her umbrella menacingly in the face of the guard and shouted: 'Why didn't you stop before, you fool? We've just passed some of the finest mushrooms I've seen in years!'

117

SALT AND PEPPER

ENGLAND, 1863

Mr Salt was one of a group of railway traffic officers who first promoted the idea of the railway companies organising and bidding for their own freight-carrying contracts.

Before Mr Salt arrived on the scene, middle men, such as Carver & Co., Weavers, Crowley and the famous firm of Pickfords, who had been carriers by road and canal, dominated the trade, and passed on to the rail only those bits of business they either didn't want themselves or couldn't cope with.

In addition to Mr Salt, the Midland Railway, quite by chance, employed a Leeds-based manager called Mr Pepper, and at various railway meetings of the day there were endless jokes as to Pepper and Salt being mustered.

The sherry-and-sandwich luncheons were incomplete without the appearance of these two condiments. Mr Salt was a man with a very cadaverous countenance and he'd first been employed by the railway as a scarer. Before the days when compartments could be reserved, this was vital if the railway's own officials were not to be disturbed by ordinary members of the public while travelling on their own railway. The permanently ill-looking Mr Salt was ordered to tie up his head with a handkerchief, and sit gloomily by a window. Few ventured to enter where such evidence existed of a fellow passenger at the point of death.

UNHEALTHY JOURNEY

ENGLAND, 1863

Having researched the subject at great length, and based on the best scientific advice available, Dr Walter Lewis, the medical officer of the London Post Office, travelled across England by train in 1863 to try to understand the effects of railway travel on humans.

Following his lengthy journey, he issued his report and concluded that 'railway travel has little, if any, injurious effect on healthy, strong, well-built persons, if the amount be not excessive, and if they take moderate care of themselves'.

But, after being shaken about on his own journey, he concluded that 'persons who take to habitual railway travelling after the age of 25 or 30 are more likely to suffer internal convulsions and potential damage to bodily organs than those who begin earlier, and the more advanced in age a traveller is, the more easily is he affected by this sort of locomotion. Weak, tall, loosely-knit persons, and those suffering under various affections, more especially of the head, heart, and lungs, are very unsuited for habitual railway travelling.'

LUGGAGE ON THE ROOF

SCOTLAND, 1865

In the early days of the railway, conductors were in charge of all passenger trains to Scotland. They were senior to ordinary guards, and at first they were given the job of travelling on trains between London and Glasgow, but, in 1865, through a joint recommendation between the Scottish Central Railway and the Caledonian Railway, it was agreed they should also travel between Euston and Perth.

While the ordinary guards were responsible for the brake vans, the conductor was given special responsibility for the luggage, and in early days had to complete a form for every package. The smartest guards were generally selected as conductors. A Mr Preston, who ended his career as stationmaster at Carlisle, had, in his youth, been one of these conductors, and he had some extraordinary tales of the perils of travelling with luggage on the roof.

The system was to strap the luggage down under heavy tarpaulins, but this did not always guarantee that one's luggage would arrive safely at one's destination – far from it, in fact. On a single never-to-be-forgotten journey Mr Preston remembered watching in horror as one carriage roof-load of luggage was knocked off by a low bridge; then as they went round a long slow bend, three large trunks slid from the roof into a muddy field by the side of the tracks. Towards the end of the journey two carriage roofs were set on fire when sparks from the engine ignited the tarpaulins.

It was sheer good luck that the light from the flames was noticed in time for the train to stop and the fire to be put out before any lasting damage was done.

Mr Preston is recorded as saying:

I had the satisfaction of seeing this roofing of luggage, a relic of old coaching days, gradually but entirely dispensed with, the manager agreeing to my recommendation to adopt the plan of a separate luggage compartment in the centre of the passenger carriages.

SUNDAY SCHOOL ROBBER
AMERICA, 1866

America's earliest train robbery occurred at Seymour, Indiana. It was an extraordinary robbery in two respects – first because, despite the wild lawlessness of the western United States at the time, no train robbery had ever occurred before, and second, because the man behind the felony was a religious leader and Sunday school teacher!

His name was John T. Chapman, a respected resident of Reno. Tall and slender, in his late thirties, he had an angelic expression. Unfortunately his expression changed a great deal whenever he thought about the gold rush at nearby Comstock Lode, which was daily disgorging vast riches of gold and silver ore, creating multimillion-dollar fortunes. Chapman, like many others who were only onlookers at this bonanza, longed for some share in the wealth. However, if he wanted a haul of gold, he knew the best way to get it was to concentrate on the trains that hauled the stuff away from the mine.

As time went on, Chapman took closer note of these operations. He then persuaded six friends to come in with him on a daring operation to rob a gold train. Time and place were set, after consideration and careful planning, for the late night of 5 November 1866, near a large rock quarry close to the town of Verdi, then a rugged logging community 11 miles (17.7km) west of bustling Reno.

On the morning before the robbery, . Jones, a member of the gang, enquired at the desk of the Capitol House in Reno and was handed a telegram from San Francisco. He scanned its lines with a furtive grin. The message read: 'Send me 60 and charge to the account of J. Enrique.' This was a code that confirmed that the gold was to leave by train the next day and that the bandits would have six men to contend with in robbing the express car.

Jones passed the word to his associates and final preparations were soon underway. They took their horses and ammunition and rode separately to their selected rendezvous, an old mine tunnel. They spent the day and evening mapping final plans, for the train, they knew, was not due until midnight. Two hours before train time, they put on their gun belts and rode in the moonlight to a nearby station, where they would board the train and ride as far as a certain culvert, the exact spot chosen for the hold-up.

The train, with its ornate wood-burning engine painted bright red, puffed its way into the station and stopped to take on a few items of freight. Standing alone on the station platform, the conductor watched as the last crate was lifted aboard. As the wheels started, he swung onto the steps of a coach. Looking ahead at that moment, he was surprised to see the figures of three men climbing aboard the front platform of a baggage car, which was directly behind the express. The conductor, whose name was Marshall, thought they were tramps, and hurried through the carriage, intending to order them off before the train had picked up speed.

The three meanwhile had made their way back through the luggage van to its front platform. As Marshall stepped out on to the platform, he found himself staring into the muzzles of revolvers held by masked men. 'Get back in there,' one of them commanded.

The conductor backed away into the van, losing sight of the armed men for a few seconds. In that instant he decided to take the risk of pulling the bell cord that would signal the engineer to stop, but found that the bandits had already cut the cord. Yet, to his surprise, the train suddenly slowed down anyway and almost immediately came to a complete stop. Returning to the open platform at the end of the van, Marshall leaned out and saw two of the same bandits on the ground, edging their way between two carriages. What he did not know then was that two more men had crept silently over the tender, piled high with split logs, jumped into the cab and forced the driver to stop. 'We're cutting you and the first carriages from the train,' they told him.

Marshall could hear heavy pounding and realised that someone was already at work trying to uncouple the carriages. Any resistance would be folly with a gun levelled at his head. So his thoughts turned to the danger facing the passenger coaches if their brakes were not applied, since the train was on a gradient. Once the engine had been de-coupled there would be nothing to stop the carriages rolling away down the hill. Then he felt a sharp forward lurch, and the driver realised that the work of uncoupling the carriages had been done.

'Now run your engine and the carriages away,' one of the gunmen commanded. 'We'll tell you where to stop.'

The driver, sitting beside his fireman, realised the danger of the situation. Speaking calmly despite the risks he knew he faced, he pointed out that the rest of the train was on a gradient and that he must signal the crew to set the handbrakes or the uncoupled passenger cars would come rolling towards them and finally crash into them.

'We'll handle that,' the taller of the bandits snapped, but the driver was not to be deterred from doing his duty. He whistled the signal to apply the brakes, and the guard further back in the train knew what to do. The armed pair swore angrily, warning against any further disobedience. 'Now get moving,' they ordered, and the driver ran his engine and the first of the carriages to the quarry, only a short distance away. There he was told to stop, and his eyes, following the beam of the locomotive light, saw close to the tracks a lone man and half a dozen saddled horses.

Driver and fireman were ordered to leave the cab and climb down, followed by the bandits still pointing their guns. Driver and fireman were told to stand aside and remain quiet. One of the gunmen kept them covered while the other began dragging pieces of timber from the roadside, and dropping them across the tracks to stop the coaches should they get out of control and roll down the hill.

Then, as the driver and his fireman looked on, they saw three men with guns running to the door of the carriage containing the gold. 'Open up and come out,' one of them called. 'Do as we tell you.' A moment later the driver saw the carriage door slide open and the staff jumped clear. The man guarding the driver and fireman then directed them to walk to the narrow mail compartment, which was then locked.

Then came loud sounds of hammering as the robbers broke into the boxes filled with gold. The gold was loaded on to horses, and minutes later the American West's first train robbery was over.

In the weeks that followed, FBI agents kept an eye on the gambling dens of Reno, where it was soon obvious that the tall Sunday school teacher had suddenly come into a great deal of money.

Before long six men had been identified as being too rich for their own good. They were arrested and soon began to implicate each other. Some of the gold was recovered, but most was hidden away in shallow holes dug out in the desert. Each of the men was sentenced to 20 years in prison, but much of their gold was never recovered and still lies hidden where it was buried all those years ago.

MAD DOCTOR

AMERICA, 1866

A businessman based in New York received a letter from his solicitor just before Christmas inviting him to a very important meeting in Chicago. 'If you don't attend you may miss something that could be enormously to your advantage,' said the letter. The businessman decided to make the trip. He travelled on 23 December and, after rushing to the station through the snow on the morning of that day, found he'd missed the train he intended to catch and had to wait several hours for the next.

At last he boarded the train and made himself comfortable in a first-class carriage, in which there was only one occupant beside himself. This was a little man, well dressed but with disordered hair and what the businessman later described as a curiously glittering and restless look in his eyes. As soon as the businessman had settled in, his fellow traveller spoke.

'A merry Christmas to you!'

'The same to you,' said the businessman.

'Why bless me,' said the little old man, 'you haven't anything to keep you warm on this bitter day. Allow me to offer you one of my travelling wrappers.' With that he took from his side a rolled-up rug, unrolled it and, taking a small mahogany box from inside it, threw the rug to his companion.

The businessman thanked the stranger and settled down to read his paper.

'I like to have a comfortable face opposite me,' said the old man.

'Why's that?' said the businessman.

'Why, the grand experiment, you know,' came the reply.

'What grand experiment?'

'Oh nothing, nothing.'

'Are you a freemason?' asked the old man.

'No I am not,' came the slightly irritated reply.

'Well you should be,' said the old man. 'Because you would then know that they have a sort of secret.'

'Well I knew that already,' said the businessman.

'Really,' came the reply. 'Well you are the most extraordinary man. I have a secret too and that's my grand experiment.'

'Well as it's a secret I suppose you won't tell me what it is.'

'Oh I will. It is simply to discover what are the different feelings of different persons on different occasions.'

'I should hardly call that an experiment.'

'Wouldn't you,' came the reply, 'well to tell you the truth I don't know myself whether I'm quite justified in calling it an experiment. But enough of that. May I ask where you are travelling to?'

'Chicago.'

'You have friends there?'

'None, I'm afraid.'

'Then may I have the pleasure of your company at dinner when we arrive there?'

'But of course.'

The businessman and his eccentric companion then fell silent. Ten minutes later, the silence was broken by the little man.

'Do you know how many times we stop before we reach Chicago?'

'Only twice, as this is the express: at 2 o'clock and then again at 5. We should arrive at Chicago at 6.30.'

'Thank you,' said the old man, who seemed to be taking notes.

Soon the businessman fell asleep, but his dreams were troubled. First he dreamed he was being hanged; then he dreamed he was being handcuffed and that a great weight was pressing on his chest. He then woke with a start to find himself bound hand and foot with a rope passed round his neck and tied to an umbrella stand in such a way that any struggling would begin to throttle him.

The little old man was now standing over the businessman with his knee pressed firmly into his chest.

'Now I shall be able to try my grand experiment,' said the little old man. 'Now I will be able to see if the heart can be extracted while a man is alive without killing him. Twice I have failed but the stars tell me that I shall not fail a third time.'

Then, addressing the businessman directly, he said: 'If you die, you will die a glorious martyr. If you live, you and I will share the glory of this great discovery!'

The businessman could do nothing – he could not struggle and a gag prevented him shouting for help. Then the old man opened his mahogany case to reveal a set of extremely sharp-looking surgical instruments. The businessman tried desperately to remember how soon they were due at their first stop – that was his only chance of being saved.

Frozen by terror, the businessman could only watch as the old man prepared his knives and his victim. He tore open the businessman's shirt and waistcoat. He sharpened several fearsome-looking instruments. At last everything seemed to be ready to the maniac's satisfaction and he picked up a razor-sharp scalpel. The businessman, eyes agog, hardly dared to breathe. The old man tested the knife on the back of his hand. It barely touched the skin but the skin parted in a red wave. The old man pressed his finger to the businessman's chest just where the heart would be and said: 'This is how I'm going to manage it, my friend. I am going to cut a circle in the flesh in the vicinity of the heart with this knife. It will not hurt much as I intend to cut only through the skin. I will then use this –' he waved another fearsome instrument in the air '– to dig out the heart.'

The businessman said later that he wanted only to scream at this point but the gag prevented it.

The old man cut through the skin and drew his bloody circle, but the businessman – despite his terror and pain – noticed that the train was slowing down. The old man was so intent on his work that he didn't notice. Just as he finished cutting the circle through the upper layers of skin, the lights of the station flashed through the windows and, in the next confused minutes, a strange arm appeared as if from nowhere and pulled the old man away. A scuffle ensued and there was shouting and arguing, but beyond that nothing. The businessman was unconscious.

For two weeks the businessman was in a life-threatening fever, but when he recovered he learned that his assailant had once been a doctor and a surgeon. As a young man he'd married, only to discover that his wife had cancer. He had operated, but the young woman died anyway. The surgeon became insane and had been committed to a mental hospital. For decades he had tried to escape in order to perform the operation that had nearly killed the businessman on the train.

THREE TRAINS COLLIDE

ENGLAND, 1866

One of the strangest and most dreadful railway accidents happened at Welwyn in Hertfordshire in 1866. It seems almost incredible that three trains should crash into each other in a tunnel and catch fire, and that the tunnel should be left for hours a huge furnace, with flames vomiting from its mouths and leaping up through 50ft (15.2m) of rock, to pour from the air-shaft in such volume as to redden the sky – but that's exactly what happened.

Welwyn is, or was, on the Great Northern Line, between Hatfield and Stevenage, leaving it about a mile (1.6km) to the left. There was first a tunnel, a quarter of a mile (0.4km) long, known as the South Welwyn, then a deep cutting a quarter of a mile long, then a tunnel three-quarters of a mile (1.2km) long, known as the North Welwyn. The underlying geology is chalk, but just on the top of the two tunnels were spurs of much harder rock. The harder rock forms a thin layer, but the bulk of the 50 feet from the crown of the tunnel arch to the top of the shaft of the North Welwyn rose almost entirely through chalk.

A few minutes after midnight on Saturday, 9 June 1866, there ran into the south end of this tunnel a train of 38 empty coal-wagons, on its way to Hitchin. With the train were the engine driver and fireman, and a guard named Wray, who had in his brake van, unknown to the others, a friend named Rawlins, to whom he was secretly giving a

lift. The friend was in the brake van against all the rules –
something for which both men would pay dearly.

All went well with the empty freight train until it reached
the middle of the North Tunnel, just under the air-shaft,
when one of the tubes from the boiler burst, and so weakened
the power of the engine that it could not draw the load. The
driver, a man called Sizer, sent his fireman, John Kemp, to
explain to Wray the reason for the stoppage, and tell him to
go back to the south end of the tunnel and give the alarm.
This, however, the guard refused to do. On the contrary, he
suggested, as they were on an incline, that the train should
be backed down the slope out of the tunnel. To go back on
the wrong line is against all the rules of railway management,
and so the driver refused to do anything of the sort.

His plan, by contrast, was to uncouple the engine,
which was powerful enough to run by itself and, leaving
the trucks, make all haste on to Stevenage for assistance.
It so happened that the signalman at the south end of the
tunnel had advised the signalman at the north end that the
train was due. The south end signalman waited for some
time and then telegraphed his colleague at the other end
of the tunnel to try to find out if the train had passed out,
as another one was due. The signalman at the north end
wired back that the train had not passed out, but the south
man read the 'No' as a 'Yes', and shifted the signals to 'all
clear'. The down Midland goods train, of 26 heavily loaded
trucks, came along as he did so, and the driver saw the
signals change from red to white, to give him a clear run.
He dashed on into the tunnel.

Kemp, the fireman on the stopped train, had just uncoupled
the crippled engine when the Midland goods train slammed
into the guard's van and sent the empty trucks flying off the
line. Wray and the stowaway, being at the back of the stalled
train, were killed instantly. The engine was derailed, and
the trucks were thrown over on to the up line and piled up
in heaps against the crown of the arch.

With extraordinarily good luck, the driver and fireman were not killed; they escaped, though they were deeply shocked. Indeed, as if to make a moral point, the only lives lost in the whole affair were those of the rule-breaking guard and his friend. No sooner had Sizer and Kemp felt the bump of the collision in the rear of their long train than an up train roared past them. This was the Scottish meat train on its way to London. In a second it had ploughed at top speed into the wagons already piled up to the roof of the tunnel from the earlier collision. The engine dug deep into the wreckage of the other trains and added to it its own.

Miraculously, the driver and fireman were thrown clear of the wreckage. But this time the fire from the engine had ignited the oil flowing from the barrels with which the Midland train had been loaded, and flames broke out. The Midland driver and fireman ran to the south end of the tunnel; the Northern driver went off on the damaged engine to Stevenage, and the Scottish driver and fireman retreated in the same direction from the suffocating smoke and heat. Thirty-six carriages were on fire. With the draughts from either end of the tunnel and the tightly enclosed mass of combustible material the whole thing quickly became a furnace.

The flames mounted the air shaft, shooting with a deafening roar hundreds of feet into the air, and from the tunnel ends streaks of fierce flame occasionally scorched through the rolling billows of thick black smoke.

Help came, but nothing could be done. The heat was intense. The explosions of the cases and barrels carried into the tunnel on the goods train could be heard for miles around. All that could be done was to let the fire burn itself out. Meanwhile, navvies were attempting to clear the line, and 450 stood ready to begin as soon as the fire permitted. Then the Marquis of Salisbury sent his personal fire engine from Hatfield House, and this was run into the tunnel. But where was the water to come from? Amid deafening whistling and screaming, engines came backing in with their tenders full, from which the fire-pumps were fed. As one tender was emptied it was run out to make room for another, and from tender to tender the pipe was passed, while the navvies, in gangs of 14, took turns at the pumps. Slowly the fire was quenched.

At the bottom of the air-shaft it burst out again, and again more tenders were backed in, and the whole process of drowning the fire began again. Then the tenders were taken out, and cranes mounted on wagons were run in. Huge chains were wound round the burnt wreckage and, bit by bit, sometimes in small masses, sometimes in huge tangled masses, the heap of black, smouldering, half-molten twisted metal was dragged out of the tunnel. Often two engines would come puffing out of the tunnel, dragging behind them a huge catch of ironwork and charred wood. Each massive bundle seemed to consist only of springs and bolts, nuts and rails, telegraph wire and wheels, screws and crowbars, coke, coal, baked meat, wheat and flour, all jumbled up together. It was more like clearing a choked sewer than a railway. What could be unhitched or unscrewed was unhitched or unscrewed. What had to be broken up was broken up. What could not be got apart was dragged out wholesale, scraping against the sides and crown of the tunnel, and tearing up the ballast beneath the tracks.

The three trains had choked the tunnel for hundreds of yards and, as two of them were heavily loaded with goods, in places the wreckage formed almost a solid plug. Again and again the flames were rekindled by the air from the ventilation shafts, and by 12.30 on Sunday morning the county police thought they had discovered a volcano.

As the day broke and the fire sank for the last time the crowds gathered in silence at the tunnel ends. Yard by yard the wreckage was cleared away and, over the ruined engines, the gangs from each end met. Then the tough job of taking away the engines piecemeal began, and with the coming of Sunday night the line was clear and the clouds dispersed.

FARE DODGERS

ENGLAND, 1867

Despite the huge numbers of staff employed to check these things, the first decades of passenger rail services were plagued by ingenious passengers finding ways to avoid paying their fares. Ticket collectors and inspectors were everywhere; tickets were checked on the train, perhaps twice in the same journey, and at the barrier.

But still the crafty managed to slip by and, in the 1860s, it was estimated that losses to the railway companies from people avoiding paying for their tickets ran into tens of thousands of pounds each year – in today's money that would translate into several millions.

The various railway companies tried all sorts of methods to reduce this kind of fraud, but as fast as they came up with new systems the fraudsters found ways to avoid them.

One scam, uncovered on the London to Brighton line in 1867, must count as the most extraordinary ever devised to avoid paying fares. The sharp-eyed inspector who uncovered the scam had noticed that every morning on the busy up train a rather thin-faced woman in huge mid-Victorian skirts lumbered slowly on to the train, then came back two hours later on the down train looking somehow less lumbering.

Something about the woman was odd, but at first the inspector couldn't work out what it was. Then he began to notice that she travelled rather a lot but never seemed to go anywhere – or at least, having travelled on the up train, she was back on the next, or nearly next, down train. She was out and back so quickly that she could never have time to do anything in between times. So what on earth was the point of her continual journeying?

It was only when the woman tripped as she boarded a train one winter's morning that the inspector realised what was going on. As she stumbled the inspector noticed two pairs of small feet poking out of her voluminous skirts – that is, two pairs in addition to the woman's own feet. The inspector was astounded, but given the proprieties of the age he could do nothing – the idea of walking up to the woman and lifting her skirts was unthinkable. But the inspector bided his time. He let her get on the train and continue her journey. He let her come back as she usually did on the next down train. But the next morning when she arrived at the station the inspector was waiting with two female detectives. They escorted the woman into a waiting room and discovered two four-year-olds under her voluminous bustle and skirts. They were dressed in school uniform and were being taken each day to their kindergarten by the woman. The woman later confessed that she was paid a small sum each day by the children's parents – a sum considerably less than the real fare – and was able to travel free herself as the widow of a former driver. She was fined two guineas and warned that she might go to prison if she was ever caught doing it again.

GUNPOWDER CRASH

ENGLAND, 1867

A bizarre railway accident happened near Penrith, in Cumberland, in 1867. The London and North Western Railway, on its way from Lancaster to Carlisle along the very edge of the Lake District, runs through Tebay junction, Shap, famous for its granite, and Clifton, and then reaches Penrith, where tourists change for Keswick. It was along this lonely, rocky line, at about 11.20 on the night of 26 February, that a goods train, having successfully climbed the Shap incline, went puffing through Clifton in that slow heavy way peculiar to goods trains.

Amid the noise, the axle of one of the wagons broke, but neither the driver nor guard was aware of the breakdown. On went the goods train, puffing hard in the darkness, a long string of trucks with miscellaneous cargoes, some laden with salt, one laden with gunpowder. Suddenly the truck with the broken axle slipped off the rails. Before the driver could stop, another truck followed suit, then another, then another; and, as the engine slowed, the trucks towards the end of the train ran closer and forced the forward ones across on to the up line.

As luck would have it, the wagon filled with four tons of gunpowder came to a halt slap bang in the middle of the up line. Before the men in charge could do anything to give notice of the danger, they heard the roar of an approaching train on the up line. It was another goods train. The driver of that train, seeing no signal, and supposing the line clear, came along at full speed – straight into the gunpowder wagon. Instantly, there was a shower of sparks and a vast all-encompassing explosion that shook and rumbled hundreds of feet into the air and deep down into the earth.

A searing burst of flame shot up and lit the whole district. The explosion shook even the distant hills; the earth trembled as if from the shock of an earthquake. For 4 miles (6.4km) round about the windows of farmhouses were smashed; and for 20 miles (32.2km) round the roar was clearly audible. The driver and stoker were killed; the wagons and goods hurled about in all directions. From the engine fires the wagons caught light, and they burnt for hours, the heavy smoke cloud hanging over the blaze and glowing red with its reflection.

As soon as they had recovered from their terror, the four survivors – the driver and fireman of the train from the south, and the guards of both trains – took measures to stop the traffic north and south of the blockage. The explosion had occurred close to Yanwath Bridge. From there to Penrith is but a mile (1.6km) or so. The breakdown gang were soon on the spot, and by 7 o'clock the next morning the line was clear, but the wreckage piled by the side was left to burn itself out, and it took all day to do so.

ANIMAL MAGIC
ENGLAND, 1868

The rules for railway travel had to adapt according to circumstances and changes in expectations. However, as the rules developed, the problem was often that they did not always keep ahead of the realities of rail travel. Thus the business of insisting that dogs had to be paid for as if they were human passengers could lead to some absurd situations.

A London and North Western passenger guard once got himself into a terrible tangle over the rules concerning dogs and tickets. At Manchester, a collie bitch, booked for Bethesda, was placed in his charge, but by the time Chester was reached the bitch had given birth to two puppies. At Chester a consultation was held by the railwaymen, and it was decided – railwaymen traditionally being soft-hearted and sympathetic characters – to make a bed for the mother and puppies on the station premises. With some difficulty the little family was removed and put in comfortable quarters, and three more puppies were added to the number in due course.

But now came the problem of tickets. One dog had been paid for, and now there were five puppies and the original dog. Who was to pay for the extra individuals? The guard and stationmaster consulted the massive rule book (in Victorian times this was the railwayman's bible, and, in theory at least, it covered every eventuality). This particular eventuality, however, had not been covered, or at least not in the history of the London and North Western. What on earth was to be done?

The enlarged consignment could not be put on the next train until the matter was resolved. Discussions were held while the mother was provided with nourishment in her comfortable bed. Officials gathered and agendas were written out for various meetings. At last a decision was reached. The mother and her puppies were forwarded as soon as it was felt the puppies could manage the journey, the carriers and the consignee having the unusual satisfaction of delivering and receiving respectively six times the number of animals shown on the way-bill. The collie was a well-bred animal, and the puppies were described as 'five beauties'.

But how was the ticket problem resolved? Well, a special leather wallet had been made at Chester, and in it were placed five half-fare tickets with a note requesting payment from the dog's owner should he deem this 'acceptable in the general spirit and goodwill of travel'. The wallet also contained a note explaining how the collie had been looked after immediately following delivery. It was then attached to the collie's collar. History does not record if the dog's owner decided that, in a spirit of fair play, he or she should pay up.

ANTI-SMOKING

ENGLAND, 1868

The idea that anti-smoking legislation is a modern obsession is entirely wrong, or at least it is if we are to judge by the mid-Victorian directors of the Great Western Railway (GWR). They hated smoking in their trains and even in their stations. They were especially active in enforcing the by-laws prohibiting it, and prosecuting offenders.

In June 1865, the General Manager of the GWR issued special orders that no smoking was to be allowed anywhere on the company's premises under any circumstances whatever. But then, to the disgust of the GWR directors, parliament passed a law that obliged the railway companies to provide smoking carriages on their trains. This came into force on 1 October 1868. Obliged to comply, a Mr Grierson, one of the most senior and exalted of all GWR officials, ordered that only the end compartments of the carriages near the rear of the train should be designated for smoking, and as few of them as possible, and that smoking should still be rigorously prevented in the stations, goods yards and everywhere else.

Staff and passengers were outraged, and on one particular occasion there was a smoking protest. A hundred or more passengers – apparently unconnected with each other – clambered abroad an express and largely occupied three carriages at the front of the train where smoking was strictly forbidden.

They proceeded to smoke their pipes and cigars far more vigorously than they would ever do under normal circumstances. The guard found he was overwhelmed by the number of smokers, all of whom had to be ejected at the next station. Umbrellas were brandished, loud arguments ensued, the guard was at times surrounded by a sea of angry puffers and the train almost had to be taken out of service. Indeed, when it stopped at a small country station the platform porter noticed more smoke coming from the windows of the carriages than from the engine.

At last the police were called and order was restored, but the smokers had made their point, and as the years went by, smoking came to dominate trains with, by the 1950s, just one or two carriages per train designated non-smoking.

BATTLE OF THE NAVVIES
ENGLAND, 1869

Britain's roads, railways and canals are mostly the work of
Irish navvies. In the days of Ireland's greatest poverty – the
middle decades of the nineteenth century – almost everyone
who could raise the boat fare left for England, America or
Australia. Those who came to England found work in their
thousands, first on the canals and then later on the railways.

But conditions were extraordinarily harsh. Navvies
worked from dawn till dusk in summer, often in remote
regions where there was nowhere to stay at night and no
food to be had round about. The railway companies took
no notice whatsoever of the navvies' difficulties, arguing,
as one railway director put it, that 'We may have to pay
them, a nuisance in itself as they are ruffians to a man, but
we are not also obliged to ensure they have a life of comfort
and ease that would risk arousing in them an envy of
their betters.'

So the navvies slept by the tracks under tarpaulins and
in tool sheds or even out in the open, night after night for
months on end. This turned them not into a race of wild
men but certainly into a fearsome tribe – which may explain
why it was frequently necessary for the cavalry to be called
when the navvies began fighting with each other or with
other groups of navvies they met along the tracks.

The biggest navvy battle of them all occurred in the
1860s, when a large group of Irish navvies began work on

a section of railway that had inadvertently been scheduled to be worked by another group of English navvies. The two groups soon came to blows, and even the local militia could do little to stop the bloodletting: at the end of the day the Irish had routed the English, but many on both sides were seriously injured, one lay dead and at least fifty were carted off to prison. The incident did little to dispel the view held by traditionalists and the landed gentry that wherever the railway went trouble was sure to follow.

SHOOTING FROM THE TRAIN

ENGLAND, 1870

An eccentric Victorian landowner was very keen on shooting but hated all the walking involved between drives. The problem was particularly acute on his estate, as the drives were some distance from each other. He tried travelling by horse; he even tried paying four of his servants extra for carrying him round in a sedan chair. This was fine, but it was difficult to shoot from the chair itself, which was what he really wanted, so the experiment was abandoned. Horses tended to bolt at the first bang.

Early bicycles seemed to hold out the prospect of shoot travel of the highest order, but, by the time he'd ordered one of the newfangled and very expensive machines, the duke realised that it would be little use over rough terrain, needing smooth tarmac to work properly.

The duke's hatred of travel meant that when bicycles and horses and sedan chairs failed, he tried all sorts of schemes to ensure that rather than his having to travel to the birds, the birds would travel to him. He planted woods near the house and had the pheasants driven towards the terrace, where he would sit ready to shoot. He even thought that if it worked well he would sit inside the house by the drawing-room window and shoot the birds as they flew over. The crafty old pheasants were too clever to fall for that one. Most simply ran across the lawns and round the house.

Eventually he had a brainwave. If the pheasants wouldn't come to his seat, he would take his seat to the birds. He called in the leading surveyors and engineers and had a miniature railway built, complete with open carriages. He learned to drive the train and persuaded the bemused engineers to build the track so it ran from one drive to the next, even taking in odd bits of woodland on the edges of the estate that would be used only occasionally. The result was a great success. The duke had little branch lines built so he could drive in and out of dead ends, and he made sure that, ultimately, if he went far enough on his railway, he would get back to where he started. He built other branch lines off the main circuit so he could examine his pens.

After the railway had been completed the great day arrived: the first day of the shooting season. The duke went down to the platform at the front of the house and boarded his little train. At the first drive he shot, as he'd always wished, from a specially built seat at the back of the engine. He did very well and enjoyed good sport at all the subsequent drives. He wrote to his friends and invited them to come and try his new shoot. They came and were each accommodated in a small, individual carriage that was then attached to the engine where the duke himself always sat. It was, as he was to observe on many occasions, the triumph of science over nature.

MUSHROOMS IN THE TUNNEL

SCOTLAND, 1870

Victorian travellers heading along the last section of tunnel into Edinburgh Waverley would have been astonished to be told that, shortly after a new detour to the east necessitated the abandoning of the old tunnel, extensive mushroom beds were established by the side of the track. The dim, damp conditions produced an extraordinarily profitable business.

The old North British Railways tunnel got into Waverley by a tunnel under St Andrews Square and Princes Street. It was about three-quarters of a mile (1.2km) long and so steep that the engineers had to build a stationary steam engine to help drag the locomotives up the incline. Once an alternative route had been established, the tunnel and stationary engine fell into disuse. Someone approached the railway company with the idea of growing mushrooms in the tunnel. The railway company were not too exacting about terms as they knew they would be paid to carry the materials for the hotbeds in and the mushrooms out.

A visitor one cold March morning found a huge fire burning just inside the lower mouth of the tunnel to take the chill off the air. The old up line was kept clear for mushroom beds; the down line had an engine on it to carry the workers as well as fertiliser, stock, produce and soil in and out. Conditions in the tunnel were so good from an agricultural point of view that tunnel mushrooms were always on the market each year well before imports from warmer foreign climes.

'THEY'RE AN INSEK'

ENGLAND, 1870

Frank Buckland, the Victorian naturalist, inventor and for many years Chief Inspector of Her Majesty's Fisheries, had a house full of animals. As a boy at Winchester school he kept hares and frogs and tortoises, mice, rats and even eels in a bath. By the time he'd reached middle age he had a house in London filled to bursting with live, dead, caged, uncaged, dying, stuffed and pickled animals from all over the world.

A visitor was as likely to meet a monkey or an armadillo on the stairs as a cat or a dog. For years, a dead gorilla languished in a large barrel filled with rum, while a giant sunfish sprawled in a vast saucer of formaldehyde. In the basement of the house, Buckland dissected any animal that had died and, generally speaking, he then cooked and ate it. One of his chief claims to fame and legacies to the modern world was the Buckland Dining Club, which still meets today. A typical menu will consist of sea slug followed by dormouse on toast.

But, in addition to his passion for animals of all sorts, Buckland had a passion for new inventions, and chief among these was the railway. As often as he was able, Buckland would take the train, and of course his favourite pets always accompanied him. This was not a problem if the pet of the moment happened to be a dog or even, at a pinch, a cat. Things were more difficult when, as usually happened, Buckland decided to take one or other of his more exotic charges.

Buckland's most famous journey began, as he later recalled, on a foggy autumn morning when he presented himself at St Pancras station ticket office. Buckland was taking with him on the journey a monkey, which proved a bit of a stumbling block to the booking-office clerk, who carefully went through the schedule of charges for the carriage of animals.

'Cows is horses,' at length said the booking-office clerk, 'and so is donkeys. Cats is dogs and fowls is likewise and so is monkeys. That 'ere animal will have to go as a dog.'

'And what about this?' said an indignant Buckland, pulling a tortoise out of his pocket.

Once more the schedule was perused.

'They are nothing,' said the clerk with some scorn after a few moments. 'We don't charge nothing for them. They're an insek.'

THE END OF BROAD GAUGE

ENGLAND, 1871

When the Great Western Railway decided at last to adopt the narrow gauge that was standard on the rest of the railway network, the company had to rip up all the old broad-gauge track. They decided to do it on a special one-off journey. The system adopted was to divide the line into lengths of about 4 miles (6.4km) for each day's work, each length being subdivided into quarter-mile (0.4km) sections, each entrusted to a gang of about 20 platelayers. A long train of broad-gauge vans was provided at the Hereford end of the line, the vans being fitted up with sleeping accommodation for the men, a travelling office for the engineers, blacksmith's shop, stores and temporary kitchens.

At the start of each day this train was worked through the length to be narrowed, stopping every quarter-mile to disembark a gang of platelayers with their tools and food for the day, before finally coming to rest at the end of the length. The narrowing was started by each gang first thing in the morning and in about four hours had been completed sufficiently to permit the passing of a narrow-gauge engine, very slowly and cautiously driven, over the newly placed rails. Up ahead the last ever broad-gauge train moved over track that would soon be gone forever.

By evening the length was completely finished, packed with ballast and in good running order.

Then commenced the operation of loading up the men and tools into a narrow-gauge train, which carried them forward to the end of the length, where the broad-gauge train of vans was awaiting them. Next followed a little miscellaneous cooking, a well-earned supper and an early bed among the straw in the vans, in preparation for another day's work, which would start at 4 o'clock the next morning.

EXTRAORDINARY ESCAPE

AMERICA, 1872

One dark, foggy night, as the express pulled out of Chicago at about 9 o'clock, the guard warned the driver to run slowly through a deep cutting about 5 miles (8km) from the station. 'All right,' he answered, but he was a notoriously fearless driver, who enjoyed nothing in the world better than a swift dash through the roaring tempest, and the guard was worried that he would take no notice of the order.

They got up a good head of speed on the early part of the journey, but the guard was now, if anything, even more worried than before. With the thick fog and the intensely dark night he knew that if there was a problem on the track, or if anything went wrong in any other way, the driver would have no time to react. And then there was that steep cutting, which always worried him.

The driver began to pick up speed and, though the guard went forward twice to warn him, he seemed unable almost to take any action to slow down. The guard later reported that, in the fog, the whole journey began to take on a dreamlike quality – an impression that was strengthened by the curious inability of the driver to do anything other than gradually increase his speed.

As the train reached the steep cutting it was going full pelt, but at least here in the steep-sided ravine the fog had lifted. Then, hardly believing his eyes, the guard saw it – a huge boulder was crashing down the side of the ravine and would almost certainly hit the train. The boulder, which must have been 15ft (4.6m) across, seemed to be moving in slow motion and at the speed the train was now travelling there was no way they could stop in time. But somehow the sense that nothing could be done reconciled the guard – as he later said – to his fate. There was nothing he could do but wait for the inevitable collision. Then, as train and boulder were about to collide, the guard watched in astonishment as the boulder seemed to hit a ridge about 20ft (6.1m) above the track, and the jolt imparted by the ridge, combined with the huge momentum of the boulder, threw it into the air and clean over the engine. Indeed, there was a point at which the guard was able to look out of the window and see the massive rock suspended as it were in mid-air above the train.

In later years he always said that the sight of that boulder missing his train as if by a miracle had almost – but not quite – made him believe in God.

STEPHENSON'S GAUGE

ENGLAND, 1872

It was in mid-May 1872 that the last broad-gauge passenger trains ever to run finished their journeys. It was a Saturday night, 11 May, when the gauge favoured by Stephenson himself finally slipped into the long oblivion of history. The very last broad-gauge train left New Milford at about 9.15pm. A special engine followed the train with Inspector Langden aboard, and it was his job to distribute notices to all concerned on the route stating that all broad-gauge stock had been removed and would never be used again.

By the Monday, narrow-gauge track had replaced the old line, and new trains were carrying passengers along the old route. Despite the fact that the last broad-gauge journey took place in the dark of late evening and night, many gathered to watch a journey that signalled the end of an era, and there was a great deal of anger from those who had always believed that the broad gauge was better – because more stable – than narrow.

NOT AMUSED

ENGLAND, 1872

In 1872, the Queen left Windsor on 14 May, accompanied by Prince Leopold and Princess Beatrice, as well as the Marchioness of Ely and Viscount Bridport. The driver had been given special instructions to work his locomotive with the utmost care, particularly when negotiating bends and when slowing down or accelerating.

This had nothing to do with Queen Victoria, who usually loved bowling along at maximum speed. No. It was all down to Prince Leopold. A special saloon, complete with a specially built invalid bed, had been added to the train for him. The Prince was carried into the station on a surgical couch on the back of a horse and cart and then carried by several retainers to the saloon; he was suffering from a slight sprain of the knee, but was behaving as if he was a badly injured war hero.

The train arrived safely at Wigan, where it stopped for the night with the passengers sleeping on board. The stationmaster, proud as Punch at the presence of his royal visitors, patrolled along the platform in the dead of night. He did not expect for a minute to see or hear anything of the royal travellers, and was astonished to find John Brown (the Queen's gillie) walking up and down in his kilt and little else, muttering to himself and apparently shouting and barking at phantoms, for no one else was about. The stationmaster asked Mr Brown if everything was all right.

Brown roared back: 'No. It isn't all right. I'm checking the wheels. The Queen says the carriage has been shaking like the devil!' And with that he stalked off still cursing and muttering.

When the stationmaster later spoke to the driver, he was told that the journey had been as smooth as it was possible for such a journey to be. 'The shaking and racket was probably just Prince Leopold complaining about everything and falling out of bed,' said the driver.

NO JOB FOR A TOFF!

ENGLAND, 1873

The Duke of Buckingham, who also happened to be, among a string of glorious titles, Marquis of Chandos, was once thought to be applying for a job as a railway porter and was turned down, despite the fact that he was a director of the company!

The man who told the tale was in charge of the station at the time. It was a freezing morning and few people were about. As if from nowhere, a slovenly-looking man entered the office and asked if he could see the stationmaster.

'The stationmaster is out,' came the reply. 'I am his deputy.'

'But I wanted to see him,' said the visitor.

'No doubt; but he is out.'

'But I particularly wanted to see him.'

'Yes, many people do; but I know what you want – you want a job – a job on the line. I may at once tell you, you won't do – you're altogether too short for any job, whether porter or guard, and I believe from the look of you that your education is wanting.'

'Perhaps then,' said the stranger, 'you will give the stationmaster my card, and say I should have liked to have seen him.'

The deputy stationmaster looked at the card. It read: 'The Marquis of Chandos.' The deputy stationmaster shook in his shoes, and wondered how soon his dismissal would be announced. He peeked out through the door of his office on to the platform where the marquis was apparently quite contentedly waiting for the next train. So this was the legendary marquis who spent every minute he could travelling by train.

In fact, the marquis was on his way to a very important meeting of the railway company. The Board was to decide who was to become its new chairman – in the event the vacant position was offered to the Marquis of Chandos and accepted by him, his Lordship taking the opportunity of saying that he highly appreciated the compliment of being elected chairman, though he had just been told, on the good authority of a highly experienced railway official, that he was not fit to be a porter! The deputy stationmaster kept his job.

RUNNING ON WOOD

AMERICA, 1873

The vast natural resources in the United States meant that finding fuel for locomotives was rarely a problem – wherever the trains went, local fuel was usually available in abundance. However, getting the right sort of fuel was sometimes a problem. In some areas, coal was in short supply and, rather than transport the stuff hundreds, perhaps thousands of miles, the railway company owners decided they would build many of their engines to run on wood. The great advantage of this was that across the vast distances of the western United States timber could be harvested all along the route.

This all sounds fine in theory, but as an English visitor to America discovered in 1873, it could have bizarre consequences. He was journeying through a remote region and had been enjoying the splendid view from the window, reading a little and sleeping a great deal, when he noticed that the train was slowing down. Expecting a station, he thought no more of it. But when the train stopped dead right in the middle of nowhere he began to wonder what on earth was going on. The Englishman immediately feared a breakdown and worried that he might be stuck in the middle of nowhere for days. But then he heard voices and, looking out of his window, saw the conductor and guard walking along the track shouting up at the passengers, many of whom were already beginning to jump down on to the tracks.

At last, the two railway employees reached the Englishman's part of the train and he heard what they were saying: 'Time to wood up, folks!'

It was then that the Englishman realised what was happening. The passengers were collecting wood from a huge woodpile and throwing it into the tender. When he expressed his astonishment to the conductor, it was explained that wood was abundant along the route but that since it burned quickly the train had to stop regularly to fill up again with fuel, and it was far quicker if all the young strong male passengers gave a hand. If the driver and fireman had to do it all on their own, the train might be delayed for several hours.

And thus it continued throughout this part of the Englishman's journey – the train stopped pretty regularly and the passengers happily jumped down and joined the refuelling team.

In England passengers would have been outraged at the idea of helping out in this way, and even if they had agreed they would expect to be paid for their labour. In America, by contrast, it all seemed to be accepted as part of the pioneering spirit.

GLADSTONE
CARRIED AWAY
SCOTLAND, 1873

Punctuality was treated like a religion in some railway companies. The Southern Region was famous for its obsessive desire to ensure trains left and arrived on time, and the same was true of the Scottish railway companies. Punctuality took precedence over pretty much everything except safety, and even royalty might be left behind if they were a minute late for a train.

One of the most amusing and bizarre examples of this sort of thing occurred at Lockerbie station. Prime Minister Gladstone had visited the town and been shown the sights. He'd stayed for several days as part of a lecture tour, but was due to leave on the 11 o'clock train for London. Every local worthy from miles round about had gathered to see the great man off: banners were waved, breakfast was laid out on tables on the platform, and the mayor and aldermen of the town made lengthy speeches of gratitude.

Gladstone himself was due to give a carefully prepared speech, and he stood on the steps of his train ready to deliver it. Unfortunately, the local worthies were queuing up to make their speeches and the last of them simply went on too long. But at last it was Gladstone's turn. He had just begun to speak – standing in the open door of one of his carriages – when the driver of the train looked at his watch, saw it was time to go, knew the rules about being late and set off.

The good citizens of Lockerbie could only stare as the great statesman was carried off, his carefully prepared speech delivered only to the wind. To give him his due, Gladstone did not dive into the safety of his compartment until the train was well out of the station. Presumably he wanted the local people to realise that, even though they could not hear his speech, he had at least continued to deliver it, apparently oblivious to the fact that every word was lost on the wind.

THE DOG SHOW
ENGLAND, 1875

A clerk who came on duty at the parcel office of a Manchester station in the middle of the day had not been long at the counter when a furious passenger appeared there and asked whether a dog that he had previously brought to the office, to be sent to the Liverpool Dog Show, had been despatched to Liverpool by the 11.15am train, as had specifically been requested.

The clerk looked over the entries in his book, and, finding the dog duly entered for the train named, told the passenger that it had been sent. In response the passenger shouted at the top of his voice: 'It's a damned lie!' Somewhat nettled at this outburst, the clerk explained that he could produce the porter who had put the dog into the train, when he was startled by the passenger asking: 'Young man, can you explain how it is that when I got home I found that very same dog you claim to have sent to Liverpool was sitting on my doorstep?'

This appeared so impossible that the clerk immediately dashed off to get the porter who was responsible for putting the dog into the train, and, on finding him on the platform, bellowed: 'Oi, Charlie, did you take a dog for the Liverpool Show to the 11.15am?'

'Yes, I did; what about it?'

'Well, there's a gentleman in the office who says that when he got home he found the dog sitting on the doorstep.'

'Did he, now? Well, I'm not surprised.'

'But how could that be if you sent it off by the 11.15?'

'Well, you know, it was like this. When the man brought the dog to the office, it was in a hamper, and he had so much to say about it that Cook (another porter) and I thought we'd like to look at it. So we opened the hamper, and no sooner had we got the lid up than the little beggar jumped out, and bolted through the door, with Cook and I after it as hard as we could go. We followed it down Hunts' Bank and along into Deansgate, where it turned off and went over the bridge into Salford, where, although we did our best to overtake it, we lost sight of it altogether. We looked at each other in dismay, and then, a happy thought occurring to me, I said to Cook, "I'm not going back without a dog. I'll have the first dog I see", and I got a dog and brought it back with me to the station, and that dog's gone to Liverpool.'

Charlie objected very strongly to the proposal that he should repeat this story to the aggrieved customer, but finally agreed to see the sender of the dog, and make a clean breast of it. Fortunately, the humour of the situation appeared to strike the gentleman who, after administering a good-humoured rebuke to the porter, said he would bring the dog back, on a chain, for a later train, and that there was to be no mistake about sending it forward this time.

The sequel to the story is that, on the following day, a hamper containing a dejected-looking dog of uncertain breed was returned to Manchester from Liverpool, with the following endorsement on the label: 'The Secretary of the Liverpool Dog Show declines to exhibit the animal contained herein – cannot classify!'

RUNNING AWAY FROM SCHOOL

ENGLAND, 1875

Charles Scott, who later became a well-known railway engineer, fell in love with the railway system after running away from school. As well as instilling a lifelong passion for railways, that early act of rebellion also taught the young Scott a remarkable lesson about the power of the railways and the service they provided.

Scott liked his school, which was in Sherwood, near Nottingham, but with his brother – who also attended the school – he one day decided to let on that his mother was ill and that he really ought to go home.

Having explained all this to his best friend, Scott and his brother decided to make a run for home, which was 130 miles (209km) away. Scott had managed to save a sovereign, which would be enough, they thought, for the journey, so he and his best friend and his brother began to plan their escape. Late one Wednesday night they dressed in their Sunday clothes, rather than the more conspicuous school uniform normally worn on weekdays, and, at 5am, they shinned down the drainpipe from their dormitory and headed off at top speed across the fields for Nottingham station, where they intended to catch the 6am train for London. As the school was 3 miles (4.8km) from the station, that allowed an hour to get there.

The school was situated on a hill about 200 yards (183m) away from the main road, which gradually descended into a valley and then rose again to Alapperley, a hill about a mile (1.6km) off, on the way to Nottingham. Unfortunately the three boys were seen leaving the school by one of the servants, who asked a few awkward questions, but did not stop them. They reached the high road, but the conversation with the servant had slowed them down and Scott was afraid they'd miss their train. They were making good time when Scott happened to look back – he saw a man on horseback just emerging from the school lane, and clearly galloping after them. They had a head start of a mile (1.6km), but there were still three-quarters of a mile (1.2km) to run before they would reach the outskirts of Nottingham, and, unless they could do this, they were certain to be caught.

They ran as fast as they could and managed to reach the first houses on the outskirts of the town just 50 yards (45.7m) ahead of the horseman, and at once dived down a narrow alley, which had posts at the entrance to stop horses. At last they had shaken him off – or so they thought. They picked their way through the courts and alleys and back-street slums of Nottingham, instead of keeping to the direct road. They got to the station at 6.05am, and so missed their train. Worse still, there was no other train until 8 o'clock.

Knowing they were still being hunted, they managed to lock themselves in the first-class waiting room, where they consumed their only food – a huge lump of very old Christmas cake. After about half an hour they heard a man trying all the doors of the rooms along the platform and searching the station from end to end. Eventually the man tried to open the first-class waiting-room door where the three boys were hiding, but evidently concluded it had been locked up for the night and had not yet been opened, and so passed on.

At 7.57am, Scott cautiously opened the door and looked out, and, not seeing the enemy, slipped into the booking office. He bought three second-class tickets for London.

When the train entered the station they made a rush for it and managed to get into a second-class carriage. Then disaster struck – just as they thought they were safe, they saw the man who'd chased them on horseback beginning to search the train, starting at the engine.

At last he reached their carriage and the three boys thought the game was up and they'd be dragged back to school and punished. Nothing, they thought, could save them now – but they hadn't reckoned on the extraordinary power of the railway. The man spotted them and made a rush at Scott's brother, but the boy got his arms wrapped round the leg of the seat, from which no amount of tugging could apparently budge him. The man gave up and turned his attention to Scott, who leapt into the luggage rack. Meanwhile, all around the other passengers were arguing and taking sides. At last the guard, hearing a disturbance, came up and enquired what was the matter.

'These young gentlemen,' said the man, 'have run away from school, and I have been sent to fetch them back.'

'Ah! That's a bad job!' said the guard. 'But let me see, have you got a ticket?'

Scott replied that all three of them had bought tickets.

'Then,' said the guard, 'the company has entered into a contract to take you to London, and it is my duty to see that contract is carried out.'

He then turned to the man from the school and said: 'And do you have a ticket?'

The man spluttered and admitted that he did not.

'In that case,' said the guard, 'I must ask you to get off the train, which is about to be delayed.'

With that, he pushed the man out of the door, shut and locked it. He blew his whistle and the train set off for London. The three boys watched the man receding into the distance, astonished at the power of a simple railway ticket. They were eventually punished when they returned to school, but the guard's reaction to their appearance on the train stayed with the young Scott, and he grew up with a devotion to the railways that lasted right through his working life.

MAD MANOEUVRES

ENGLAND, 1875

Lecturing at a meeting of the Society of Locomotive Engineers, Sir John Aspinall once told the story of an exciting experience that regularly befell him in the early 1870s, when he was firing on passenger engines for the London and North Western Railway.

When the London expresses ran into Crewe, it was usual to call out an extra engine whenever the load was heavy. This extra engine helped the train along as far as the top of a big incline at Tring. Then it was detached, and the manner of detaching was one that made many a railwayman's hair turn grey. The procedure was as follows: as the train drew near to the signal box at Tring, the fireman of the extra engine climbed over the tender and unhooked his engine from the other. Then, the disengaged extra engine ran over the points just ahead, and backed into a siding, waiting there while the London express ran past, afterwards emerging to return to Crewe in readiness for further work. Meantime, the express never stopped, or even slowed appreciably, and there were always breathless, exciting seconds of suspense while the extra engine ran clear.

There was absolutely no mechanical protection should anything have gone wrong, and such a method of working would be considered completely insane today, yet the extraordinary procedure was carried out day after day for years on end.

AGAINST ALL THE ODDS
ENGLAND, 1876

To travel on the Settle to Carlisle line in the North of England – a line completed in 1876 – is to experience one of the most extraordinary journeys it is possible to make by rail. Not, it must be added, because there is anything inherently remarkable about the engines on this line, their speed or about the other passengers: no, in this case the extraordinary fact is that there is a railway there at all.

The difficulties of building the Settle to Carlisle were, at the time the line was built, virtually insurmountable. Most experts said it simply couldn't be done, but they reckoned without the resourcefulness of those early railway engineers.

The Settle to Carlisle line is just over 70 miles (113km) long, but it took over seven years to make and cost over £3million – about 20 times the cost of building a comparable length of line at that time anywhere else in the country.

Difficulties dogged the railway engineers almost from the day the railway was planned. When it was being staked out, the chief engineer and his men were snowed in for weeks at the Blea Moor Inn, one of the most remote pubs in Britain. For three weeks the snow fell continuously, until it lay 7½ft (2.3m) thick, and it was only by driving a tunnel through the snow to the road that the men, who had been living solely on eggs and bacon, got water from a horse-trough to drink.

The making of the line was a battle, with every inch gained only after a massive struggle. Along its whole length there was not a single level piece of ground big enough to build a house on, and the line's embankments, cuttings and tunnels had to go over, under or through almost every variety of rock known to the geologist.

Along the southern part of the line there is a section through boulder clay, the most unsatisfactory of all materials for the railway engineer – one minute it was a thick soup that had to be removed by bucket, the next it was an unyielding rock. One day it was so hard it took tons of explosive to shift; the next, after heavy rain, it turned to glue.

Further on, the engineers hit the diamond-hard rock of the outlying flank of Whernside, Blea Moor, where 2,000 men worked for four years or more on embankment, tunnel and viaduct, with winds so high at times that the bricklayers could not work for fear of being blown from the scaffold.

In driving the first opening for a tunnel, only four men were able to work in one place, using the technology then available. But to compensate for this, the tunnellers not only bored from each end, but shafts were dug down from the top, each shaft giving two more faces to work at. At Blea Moor there were seven shafts, some of them 50ft (15.2m) and more deep. This meant an opening was made for 16 gangs of men, working night and day, four of the shafts being eventually left as ventilators. Once the initial tunnel had been opened up, the hole was enlarged sufficiently to allow the arch to be put up in brickwork, the space behind being filled in with loose rock. Then the excavation of the tunnel was continued down to the level of the rails, and the sides and floor put in. Vast amounts of dynamite were used and, as this could not be sent by railway, it had all to be carted from Carlisle or Newcastle at a cost of £200 a ton – a huge sum at the time. It was estimated that 33,000 navvies were employed in total before the Carlisle to Settle was finally complete and the first passengers were able to travel on this remarkable line. Most knew little or nothing of what had been endured to enable their journey to take place.

SNATCHBURY

ENGLAND, 1879

Men have always been fascinated by steam trains. Even before they were consigned to the long oblivion of history, moves were afoot to keep at least some of them running on preserved lines. Women rarely become so passionate about steam, but dogs occasionally share their master's passions.

For several years there was, for example, a bright little English terrier that travelled regularly from King's Cross to Doncaster seated on the toolbox between the driver and the fireman. Hail, rain or sunshine, the dog would be seen sticking to his post, while the engine dashed along at full speed and the wind brushed out the little dog's coat until it looked as if it were made of bristles. Several other dogs are recorded as inveterate train travellers, but few are able to match the fame of the near-legendary Snatchbury.

Snatchbury was known as the prince of drivers' dogs, his adventures reported regularly in *The Times* and other newspapers. His story began when, out of the blue, he turned up one day at Euston, dodging about on the platform, evidently looking for a friend. Having chosen his platform, the dog sat down and looked questioningly out along the track. A train came into the station right by the platform where the little dog sat waiting, and the driver, known as 'the Duke', from his aquiline nose, caught sight of the dog and called him. The little rough-haired, small-headed lump of light-brown doggyness jumped on to the footplate, and scrambled up to the back of the tender. Twenty minutes later, off went the train, and with it went Snatchbury, as he came to be christened.

For ten years afterwards, by night and day, through fog and sunshine, Snatchbury stuck to the Duke, and, with his shaggy hair blown back so as to show his white teeth, hardly ever missed his engine. Every day he would come on duty and race down the engines in the shed till he found the right one, and if it had been moved he would leap and whine till it was pointed out to him.

One day he came too late. His favourite driver was just going out of the station. Snatchbury was distraught, but he was also an observant dog. He waited till the next engine going the same way started, and then he jumped on that train and went to Rugby, where he changed engines to Bletchley, and there caught up with the Duke!

Snatchbury's intelligence was remarkable. He learned the signals, and could tell whether they were up or down, or red or green, and if a red light was shown ahead he would announce the fact with a warning bark. Even the fog-signals he came to know the meaning of, and he would bark to announce the dangerous ones! In fact, Snatchbury took an intelligent interest in all that he came across, and seemed never to forget what he saw. And he was a kind-hearted dog, too. His face was often seen by passengers and railway workers alike on the engine at Euston, leaning over and looking along the train; and, if he noticed a strange dog being put into the brake van by the guard, he would jump down and run in to the new arrival to have a quick sniff and a tail-wagging session before returning to his place at the engine!

Then one terrible night a signalman at Harrow made a mistake, and showed the line as being all clear when a goods train was in the way. On came the Duke in obedience to the signal, full speed into the trucks he could not see. He was killed instantly. Snatchbury was hurled off with him, but was unhurt. The dog's grief was heartbreaking. At the funeral the dog walked beside the coffin. Back at the drivers' common room, the Duke's boots were placed by the fire, as though ready for him when he came back. And with his nose between his paws poor Snatchbury waited there for the master he was never again to see. After a time Snatchbury recovered somewhat and took to another driver; but it did not last long. When he died some years later Snatchbury was taken to the taxidermist, stuffed and put into a glass case. His current whereabouts are unknown.

AMIABLE LUNATIC
FRANCE, 1880

To travel with a lunatic is not an agreeable experience, but travel long enough and far enough by train and you will certainly encounter the mad, the bad and sometimes the dangerous to know. An English businessman who travelled to the South of France and back towards the end of the nineteenth century recorded his meeting with what he described as an amiable lunatic; the sort of person who, though not quite dangerous, is vaguely alarming and seems to delight in doing things that are unnerving, to say the least.

Having reached Marseilles and conducted his business, the Englishman toured the city for a few days. In an account of his adventure written towards the end of his life, and published anonymously, he remembered the pleasure of Marseilles:

It is such a wonderfully bright, busy, bustling place. There is a Moorish look about the old Southern town, and the people one sees walking about the dusty streets are of the most polyglot description. The turban and the fez are quite common, and Oriental and European languages are spoken almost indiscriminately. My friends were kind, the weather was superb, and altogether I had a delightful time.

Monday was the day set for his departure, but he spent much of it wandering the city on foot, to the extent that by the time he arrived at the station he was dog-tired and looking forward to a good sleep in his compartment on the way back. But it was not to be. He reached the St Charles station just in time for the *rapide* train to Paris.

The travelling Englishman takes up the story of what happened next:

The spick-and-span conductor of the sleeping car – for the International Sleeping Car Company had one of their luxurious vehicles on the train – handed me a telegram from a French friend who was going to join the train at Dijon at about 4 o'clock the next morning. He remarked, at the same time, that it looked as if I were to have the compartment – with berths for four – all to myself that night.

Throwing my weary body on the seat, I waited for the train to set off. Just then I heard voices carrying on an animated discussion in the corridor, and an instant later two ladies and an old gentleman burst into the compartment. For a moment I thought our conductor, a Dutchman, was about to plant the three of them on me in the coup for the night, which would have been awkward for me – modesty and the rules of social intercourse would have forced me, despite my exhausted state, immediately to move to another compartment.

However, the two ladies – and they were both young and pretty – put the old gentleman into a nice, cool alpaca coat and left him. After having quitted the car, they stood on the platform as the train moved out of the station. They blew kisses to the old man till we were out of sight.

It was at this point that the Englishman noticed the old man putting a large red handkerchief to his face. He then heaved three massive sighs into its voluminous folds and a pigeon appeared as if from nowhere from the folds. 'There you are, you little rogue!' he said.

The Englishman couldn't believe his eyes, but having regained his composure simply assumed that this was a practising magician. In the next moment the Dutchman – for that is what he seemed to be, judging by his accent – had opened the window of the train, shouted, 'Now go home, you bugger!' and thrown the bird into the slipstream. The magician, if that is indeed what he was, then looked across at the Englishman with a radiant smile on his face.

'Good evening, Monsieur,' he said. 'It's rather warm tonight, is it not?'

'Yes, sir, very warm indeed,' replied the Englishman.

Seeing that he was ready for a long conversation, the Englishman, who desperately wanted to sleep, tried to cut him short by saying, 'Excuse me, sir; I am an Englishman, and do not speak French very fluently. Besides, I have been walking about all day and am tired.'

But the old man took absolutely no notice and began paying the Englishman extravagant compliments about the excellence of his French.

'You are an Englishman, and I am Flemish; we both speak French, and are compelled to remain here for the next 15 or 16 hours. Why, then, we must have a good talk!'

The Englishman's heart sank – without being rude, this was going to be a very difficult situation to escape.

But then conversation was not, as it turned out, quite what the old man had in mind. He began a long rambling account of his own life.

'You must not think I have been travelling on a journey of pleasure,' he said. 'For I did not leave Brussels until Saturday, reaching Marseilles last night (Sunday); and here I am on my way back again.' Then, leaning over the table, he said in a whisper, while dramatically striking his forehead two heavy smacks with the palm of his fat hand, 'My wife's sister is ill. Do you see?'

'Yes,' said the Englishman to himself, 'I do see; she's clearly barking mad and it occurs to me that you are ill in the same way too.'

But needing no encouragement the old man continued as before.

'Those two young ladies are my nieces. They are the daughters of a bank manager who plans to vanish and I've been called in – though I am by profession a baker – to find him once he's gone.'

At this point the old man pulled out his purse and displayed a huge number of bright golden coins. 'What do you think of these?' he asked, as he extended his gloved hand. In an instant, the gold had vanished, to be replaced by a handful of gaudy-looking jewellery. He showed the Englishman numerous pieces of the most tawdry jewellery.

'A present for my wife,' said the old man. 'Well, I mean I will give them to my wife when I find her and marry her.'

By this time the Englishman was half alarmed and half amused, but he felt too tired to indulge any view of the old man for long, such was his desperation for sleep.

'What if he attacks me?' thought the Englishman, who considered asking the conductor to move him to another compartment. But the innate English desire not to cause offence kept him in his seat. The old man continued to chatter about anything and everything, speaking ever more quickly with extravagant gestures and wildly flailing arms, while the Englishman prayed that he might shut up even if only for five minutes so he could get some sleep.

But the old man was enjoying himself now. 'Have you seen the inside of my coat?' he asked. Hardly bothering to wait for an answer, he whisked off his coat to reveal an extraordinary satin lining decorated with strange hieroglyphs and bizarre markings.

'I believe this explains the inner secrets of the heavens and the secret of our world,' said the old man. 'If you know how to read it – and I don't – it will also give you all of Europe's railway timetables, including details of which trains will be delayed.' He winked at the Englishman and pulled out a horribly messy packet of sandwiches.

'Sea slug,' he said with a knowing look while tapping the side of his nose. 'Sea slug explains my great age and youthful appearance. I won't tell you when I was born lest you find me suspicious.'

He then began to tapdance and swirl about the carriage, shouting incomprehensible things about his cape and the contents of his pockets. But, after ten minutes of this odd behaviour, exhaustion clearly got the better of him, and he flopped down into the seat next to the Englishman. He then became enormously concerned about the Englishman's welfare and offered to buy him wine, brandy, a cigar, a box of handkerchiefs, a rifle and two cummerbunds. The list seemed to go on forever and grew ever more bizarre.

The train stopped at Avignon, and the Englishman stood in the corridor looking out on to the platform, viewing the movements of a number of passengers and the usual incidents of station life, so familiar and yet so strange. With an inward groan he then heard the voice of his travelling companion. Stepping back into his compartment, the Englishman saw that the old man now had a large clasp knife in one hand and in the other hand a long square bar of ordinary washing soap.

'You would like some cheese?' he said, indicating to both knife and soap, and in a moment a piece of the soap was in his mouth, and a moment later he was spitting and spluttering on the floor of the car.

'Ah, Monsieur,' he said with tears in his eyes, 'I love it but it is so strong I'm sure it is bad for me.'

By now the Englishman was thoroughly alarmed, but at the same time he felt powerless to do anything about his situation. Still he had not been able to sleep and he was so tired that he felt on the verge of hallucinating.

About then the conductor came in to the compartment and explained that a one-legged man had asked if the Englishman would mind having the upper bunk in order that the one-legged man should not have to climb to a difficult height.

The Englishman immediately realised, and with huge relief, that this was his chance to escape the attention of the old man. He agreed to move up to the upper bunk and immediately did so, refusing to come down again despite the pleas of the old man.

When he realised that his companion was not going to continue their conversation, the old man announced in a loud voice that his grandfather, the sultan, never went to bed before three in the morning and he intended to continue the family tradition. Thus, on the few occasions when the Englishman dared peep over the edge of his bunk, he saw the old man sitting on the floor, cross-legged and smoking an extremely long pipe.

The train stopped at Valence, and it was nearly midnight. It seemed ages since dinnertime, and the Englishman was hungry. Through the window he could see young men selling rolls, butter and jams from trays, but how on earth could he go out and buy these things when the madman was still sitting on the floor?

The answer came in an instant when the Englishman looked once again over the edge of his bed. Below, where the old man had been, there was nothing. A second later the door of the compartment opened and the old man appeared with rolls, butter and coffee for the Englishman, the one-legged man and himself. As he tucked into this most welcome food, the Englishman almost felt some affection for the man who had driven him to the edge of distraction.

Another man had now entered their compartment, and the old man was entertaining him with bizarre tales and dances, odd snatches of song and poetry. At one stage he also pulled up the leg of his trousers to show the newcomer a wound he claimed he'd received during the Crimean War. At last, at 3 o'clock in the morning, the old man agreed to go to sleep.

In the morning the old man was up first and he was talking to the Englishman even before the Englishman was fully awake.

'We are near Brussels,' he said. 'You must accompany me on a grand tour in my private coach.'

'No, thank you, Monsieur,' said the Englishman.

'But I'll pay, I'll pay!' came the reply.

The Englishman explained that he was meeting a friend and then going straight on to England. The old man was devastated and began to weep. The Englishman, overcome with embarrassment, shook his hand. When last he looked back along the platform, the old man had turned his extraordinary coat inside out and was sitting on a bench playing a small set of bagpipes of a type the Englishman had never seen before.

PLATFORM DOG
ENGLAND, 1880

There are many stories concerning dogs travelling alone by train. Several dogs are known to have crossed the northern wastes of Russia on the trans-Siberian railway unaccompanied, and, on occasion, dogs have accidentally hopped onto trains that have taken them hundreds of miles from home.

At Reading at the end of the nineteenth century there was even a platform dog that ran around the station with a special leather collection box tied to its back collecting money for charity. It took regular trips to London, presumably hoping to raise even more cash for good causes. It was so popular that when it died it was stuffed and put in a big glass case on the platform, and was still there well into the 1970s.

But perhaps the most extraordinary animal traveller of all was a dog that with an almost human instinct always seemed to know where he wanted to go and how to get there. He was known as Railway Jack and belonged to a former stationmaster at Lewes who, in the early 1880s, was a frequent traveller on the trains between that station and London.

Railway Jack's knowledge of the timetable was vast. He appeared to know all the trains up and down and travelled, so far as anyone could make out, for the pure love of it. He would often get out of the train at intermediate stations for a saunter in the countryside or to greet the rustic railway staff, but never missed the last train home.

A remarkable fact about Jack was that he was never known to take the wrong train. Once, when placed by a porter in the guard's van of a train that was not going to his destination, he appeared to sense in some extraordinary way that matters were not right. So he jumped out and returned to the platform waiting room until his train to Lewes arrived.

Jack travelled all over the south-east for years, visiting all the major towns and many tiny villages where there were stations. Passengers were always delighted to see him; he was adored by schoolchildren and universally missed when at the age of about 18 he died in his sleep.

THE HOUSE THAT WASN'T THERE

ENGLAND, 1881

The Victorian obsession with ghosts probably made people far more likely to see them, rather like conspiracy theorists that see conspiracies everywhere precisely because they are always looking for them. But a curious incident recorded in the files at Scotland Yard towards the end of the nineteenth century suggests that every now and then a ghost story really did have some basis in reality.

This story begins with the visit of a young woman called Agnes Wilkins and her governess to London. As their train approached King's Cross station it slowed through the smoke-blackened houses of the North London suburbs: mile after mile of mostly poor terraced houses, interspersed with the occasional more substantial dwelling.

The train slowed to a halt at a set of signals about five minutes from their destination. It was early evening and most of the windows in the houses were already lit. Then something caught Agnes's eye. She had been staring out the window, as she later explained to the police, because she had grown tired of reading her book. She saw two figures in the drawing room window of a house that seemed to have been built apart from the others. It was also much larger. In the orange light of the gas-lit room a couple were speaking to each other in what seemed to be 'heated tones'. They could be seen quite clearly through the long drawing room windows that extended almost from floor to ceiling.

They appeared to be involved in a violent argument, as Agnes explained to the police: 'They were making wild gestures with their arms, then breaking apart to walk across the room and then back towards each other. They both seemed terribly angry. Then, just as our train began to move off, I saw the man lift his hand high above his head and now his hand held a large knife and it was right above the woman's head. In that instant she cowered and tried to protect herself with her hands, but he stabbed viciously down again and again. By then we were moving out of sight as the train had continued its journey, but I was deeply upset and knew I must contact Scotland Yard as soon as I was able.'

And that is exactly what Agnes did. She and her governess called a cab when they arrived at King's Cross and asked to be taken straight to Scotland Yard. Agnes gave a lengthy statement and the police promised to investigate.

Six months later Agnes received word that no murder appeared to have been committed in the area that she had described, but the story did not end there. The police asked her to call in next time she was in London and this she did. She was escorted into the superintendent's room and told that in precisely the spot she had described there had indeed been a murder – but it had taken place 50 years' earlier. A man had stabbed his wife to death in the drawing room of their large house, just as Agnes had said. But within a year of the murder the house in which it had taken place had been demolished at the request of the family. The superintendent explained that a few months after Agnes had seen the murder, another passenger on a train into King's Cross had reported seeing precisely the same thing.

DANGEROUS PRACTICES
AMERICA, 1881

An Englishman visiting America was astonished at the
dangerous way in which some American railways were run.
On one journey he heard the sound of feet running on the
roof above his head while the train roared along at more
than 50mph (80.5km/h). On each occasion, before the train
entered a tunnel, the Englishman noticed a loud thump on
the roof overhead.

He discovered later that the practice on American trains
was to fit brake screw handles to the roofs of the carriages.
This meant that the brakeman had to run along the top
of the vehicles, applying the brakes when necessary. This
was a terrifying business in rough weather, and especially
so where there were tunnels. As a protective warning,
overhanging gantries with hanging whipcord pellets were
provided not far from the tunnels, so that the men on the
roofs were hit by the pellets and knew it was time to throw
themselves flat or be killed!

LOST TRAINS
ENGLAND, 1881

On the Settle to Carlisle line, in 1881, every device for getting through a huge snowdrift was tried in vain when the train became snowed up completely. Only the top of the engine funnel appeared above the white waste, and a passing navvy walking high up on the packed snow is reported to have used the 6in (15.2cm) of the funnel still visible as a spittoon!

Apart from the buried train, the signs that this was an extraordinarily bad storm were everywhere: stations were buried, passengers died of hypothermia and telegraph wires were so covered with ice and snow that, in places, they were as thick as a man's arm.

Elsewhere, the drifts in Cumberland were more than 40ft (12.2m) deep, and out of them were dug ten cold locomotives that had been buried for weeks. The same storm cost the Great Western £56,000, much of that the cost of having to excavate over a hundred miles (161km) of snow from 3–10ft (0.9–3m) thick, in which were buried 51 passenger trains and 13 goods trains.

During the same storm, a North-Eastern engine went northwards out of Gateshead, and began work by driving through a drift a mile and a half (2.4km) long and 14ft (4.3m) deep, before finally reaching a cutting where the snow had solidified into so compact a mass that the engine stuck fast. From the Monday morning to the following Saturday night, none of the men at work to clear the tracks was ever able to go home. They slept in their clothes in a makeshift hut. For 38 hours they were without water, except that obtained by melting the snow. It was a miracle no one died.

PONY RIDES

ENGLAND, 1882

The Eastern Counties Railway service was famous for its delays and lack of punctuality. The anecdote that best summed this up concerned a woman and her son. The boy was clearly well beyond the age at which he was entitled to a half fare, so there was a slight disagreement between the woman and station staff when she reached the end of her journey.

The ticket inspector said: 'This child is too old for a half fare.'

The woman replied: 'He may be now but he wasn't when we bought the ticket!'

But if the Eastern Counties railways were plagued by bad timekeeping they were also occasionally plagued by eccentric travellers. On one journey the guard was summoned by a passenger who claimed she could hear heavy scuffling and knocking sounds from the compartment next to hers. The noises had been intermittent but occasionally violent. She explained that she'd tried to open the door of the compartment to check that all was well, but it seemed to be locked. She'd also noticed that the blinds were pulled down, so there was no way to check that the occupants had not suffered, as she put it, 'some dreadful calamity'.

The guard suspected that the woman was actually just being nosy and was happy to use any excuse to find out what was going on in the darkened compartment, but he felt he had to at least humour her. He'd just begun to explain that some travellers liked to sleep or were simply concerned not to be disturbed when he heard a violent thud. In fact, it was so violent it almost seemed that the compartment might burst.

The guard knocked cautiously on the compartment door. There was no reply. He knocked again and said: 'Good morning. This is the guard. Are you all right?' Still no reply. Then another thud followed by loud shufflings. The guard told the woman still standing by his side that he would summon help. He returned with the ticket collector and they managed to force the door. Inside they found a middle-aged and very portly man asleep in a corner seat by the window. Filling the rest of the compartment between the two rows of seats that faced each other was a small but very nervous-looking pony.

In the instant they realised what it was, the pony kicked out its back legs and narrowly missed the guard. The door-jamb splintered under the impact of the pony's iron-shod hooves and the fat man woke up. Rather than apologise for the outrage of putting a pony on the train in this way, the man argued that his sleep had been interrupted by the guard and ticket collector. He simply would not accept that he had done anything wrong. When he and his pony were ejected at the next station, he swore the company would be hearing from his solicitors. In fact, he was never heard of again.

How he managed to get the pony on to the train in the first place without anyone noticing remains a complete mystery.

NAKED DRIVER
ENGLAND, 1886

John Brennan was one of the most unpleasant characters you could wish to meet. He had been a locomotive driver for 30 years and for most of it, so his colleagues said, he had been in a bad mood. His firemen – whose job it was to continually shovel coal into the firebox – always groaned when they realised they had been put on a rota that meant they had to work with him.

He was a short, fat, unprepossessing little man who thought he was God's gift to women and the railways. His arrogance knew no bounds, but on a fateful day in 1886, he did something so bizarre that it brought to an end his long career on the railway.

Stopping overnight at Doncaster he visited several pubs and was clearly inebriated when he finally reached his lodgings in the early hours. In those days all railwaymen drank beer – often with their lunch and when they were driving. It was certainly bad practice, but then beer was much weaker in the nineteenth century than it is today, and there are very few records of crashes or other disasters caused by alcohol.

But Brennan had to drive an early train and he must have been under the influence when he awoke that morning at 5 o'clock. Certainly his fireman later reported to the disciplinary board that Brennan was behaving very oddly as they prepared to leave the station.

All went well once they were underway, but Brennan was clearly not himself. For a start he was in a good mood and was singing at the top of his voice. But he then told the fireman he was too hot and began to take his clothes off. By the time they had gone 50 miles (80km) he was driving without a stitch of clothing on, and nothing the fireman said would persuade him to put his clothes back on.

They reached London at last and Brennan was arrested. He spent the night in the cells, insisting all the while that he had done nothing wrong, but as the magistrate later pointed out, certain elderly ladies on the platform had seen things no elderly lady should ever set eyes on. Brennan was fined, and after his railway disciplinary hearing he was sacked. This is the only reasonably well-attested example of a railwayman driving a train while completely naked.

The incident was the talk of the drivers' common room for months afterwards. Some thought that Brennan's drinks had been tampered with; others were convinced that decades of grumpiness had finally led to a sort of breakdown during which Brennan had thrown caution – and his career – to the wind.

LOVE ON THE TRAIN
FRANCE, 1886

He might have been Turkish or Greek or from North Africa. Certainly he had at least three, possibly four places of birth according to his own account, which varied according to time and circumstance. No one quite knew when he was born but Zacharie Zacharoff (who went also under a number of pseudonyms) was certainly born into poverty, probably in Constantinople in the 1840s or 1850s. He was, by all accounts, born of doubtful parentage and raised in great poverty in the dusty streets of that crumbling city. Yet half a century later he had been awarded one of France's highest honours, the Legion d'Honneur, after a life of extraordinary intrigue. But the pivotal point of his life was, without question, an extraordinary journey on the Orient Express, that symbol of pre-Great War luxury that died slowly only with the coming of luxury passenger flying.

Zacharie spent his life living off his wits – that much is known for sure. After his earliest days in Constantinople, where he may have worked as a waiter, he vanished until the 1860s, when he emerged suddenly with a wife and another name – Manel Sohar. In the 1870s he began working for an uncle's general merchant business. He then vanished again before reappearing in England, where he somehow developed a connection with an arms firm and began selling their weapons to various governments in Central and Eastern Europe.

Whenever he travelled across Europe, he took the Orient Express, and each time he did so he contacted an Albanian pimp who supplied him with a redhead – it had to be a redhead – for the duration of the journey. He became very rich and spent more and more time on the Orient Express, travelling ever more widely and selling increasing numbers of weapons. Soon the railway staff grew so used to him that they bowed when he arrived at the platform and no official at any border crossing would dare to ask to see his passport. He was treated as only the members of European royal families were treated.

Only once was he kept waiting, and that was at the beginning of what was to prove a most extraordinary journey. He was held for a few moments while waiting to board the Orient Express while a young Spanish couple were allowed through. They were Don Francisco y Bourbon, a cousin of the Spanish King Alphonso XII, and his young bride, who were setting off for their honeymoon. Zacharie was astonished at how unhappy they looked, but soon they had vanished into the luxurious carriage, which was reserved for them, and he thought no more of it.

Late that night, as the train hurtled across the dark landscape, Zacharoff heard loud and terrifying screaming. A few moments later, he opened the door of his compartment and discovered a torn, bleeding and half-dressed young and very beautiful woman, whom he instantly recognised as the young Spanish bride he'd earlier seen boarding the train. She looked straight into his eyes and said almost in a whisper, 'Save me! He will kill me!'

Then Zacharoff noticed that a short way along the corridor one of his servants was wrestling a fearsome-looking dagger from the hand of a young man who lunged and kicked like someone out of his mind. Zacharoff invited the girl into his compartment, shut the door and made her comfortable. It is said that, by the time the train reached Vienna, some three hours later, Zacharoff was in love. It was a love that was to supersede all previous loves – including redheads – and it lasted till the end of Zacharoff's life.

At Vienna, the young bridegroom was bundled away by a group of officials and taken to an asylum. The young woman went with them, and Zacharoff may have thought that was the last he would see of her. But somehow, after the extraordinary events on the train, Zacharoff and the young woman – whom he knew as Doña Maria – managed to correspond with each other and Zacharoff soon discovered that the young woman's mad husband had been escorted back to Spain.

Soon Maria became an outcast – nothing could be the fault of the Spanish royal family, so the young man's madness was blamed on the cruelty of the woman who had abandoned him. She was sent into exile and joined Zacharoff permanently on his long journeys across Europe and always on the train on which they'd first met.

As the years passed they had three children, all daughters, and Zacharoff grew ever richer. Eventually he was employed as the arms manufacturer Vickers' top man in Europe. By 1922 Don Francisco – the mad bridegroom – was still in an asylum but he was 62 and in ill health. Zacharoff was in his seventies and his name was a legend.

Zacharoff astonished the world in 1923 by buying the Monte Carlo casino for the then unheard-of sum of £1 million. At last, in 1924, Don Francisco died, after a lifetime's confinement in an asylum. Then, almost 40 years to the day after they had met on the train, Zacharoff and Doña Maria were married. Two years later she was dead. After her death Zacharoff never again travelled on the Orient Express. He was fabulously wealthy but gradually became a recluse before dying at last in 1936.

The evening following his death, in accordance with the strict instructions left in his will, two of Zacharoff's servants took the Orient Express from Paris towards Salzburg. At 2.30am precisely – the exact time Zacharoff had first met

Doña Maria – one of the two took a photograph of Doña Maria and her three daughters from his pocket, tore them into pieces and scattered them out through the window of the speeding train into the cold night air.

GENIUS OF THE IRISH

IRELAND, 1888

The Irish are passionate about horses and horse racing and when a big meet is on, sporting enthusiasts will do almost anything to avoid missing the big day.

Trains from Dublin to the Curragh were always packed on race day, but on this particular day, 18 May, the crammed train was pulling out of Dublin station when three young lads tore along the platform and jumped aboard. They'd arrived too late at the station to buy their tickets but knew that if they missed this train they'd miss the best of the day's sport. Once aboard they had a big problem. When the ticket collector appeared they would have some explaining to do – they had no tickets and would at the very least have to pay an excess fare and might even be fined.

'What on earth shall we do?' said one. 'We'll be prosecuted!'

'Nonsense,' said his friend with a knowing wink. 'We'll be fine.' Quite why he was confident he would not say, but, convinced of their friend's ability to get them out of a jam, they settled down to enjoy the journey.

When they reached the first station, at which their tickets were almost certain to be examined, the young man who'd been so sure they would be all right leapt out of his seat and ran out of the door of the compartment without a word. A few minutes later he dashed breathless back into the carriage but with three tickets held aloft.

'Where on earth did you get those?' said one of his friends.

'I went along till I found a carriage with some Englishmen in it' – they had to be English for the Irish would be too cute to fall for it – 'and I just said, "Tickets please!" and they handed them over without a murmur!'

STICKY TRACKS

AMERICA, 1888

In the eastern states of America, as was afterward true in the west when the railroad expanded into those remote regions, it was often hard for those who lived in isolated country districts to get trains to stop at their stations, and to secure other privileges upon which the growth of their settlements depended. In 1817, a little group of people had settled about a mile (1.6km) out of Medford, some 6 miles (9.7km) from Boston. They paid a visit to the offices of the superintendent of the railroad one day, with a request that he should stop the train at their admittedly tiny settlement. They argued that, once the train began to stop, the hamlet would grow first into a village, then a town and – who knows – maybe eventually a city.

The superintendent refused, point blank, simply because he believed he would lose money if he agreed to the plan. But the people of Medford refused to give up and persisted in their demands. When he remained firm in his refusal, they went away declaring they would make him stop the train whether he wanted to or not.

The superintendent took no notice of threats like this – he received them pretty regularly and often from individuals who took it as a personal affront that he would not agree to stop the train regularly at their individual farmhouses!

There was a steep incline just outside Medford, and a few days after the superintendent's meeting with the villagers, the express train driver found that as he reached the incline his wheels began to slip. Within seconds, the train had come to a full stop, and it stopped right by a group of Medford villagers.

They jumped aboard while the train driver got out to investigate the cause of the delay. He couldn't believe his eyes! The track, for nearly a quarter of a mile (0.4km) up the incline, had been smeared with – of all things – molasses.

The driver had to back his train up till he could get sufficient momentum to carry him over the hill. In the face of such persistence, there was no use in trying to run past Medford – the good citizens of that tiny hamlet got the regular stops they'd always wanted.

MOURNED BY ALL
SCOTLAND, 1890

When Jock the Perth railway dog died, he was mourned on both sides of the English Channel, and even further afield.

No one could quite remember when Jock first appeared, though it was generally agreed to be about 1890, when he was still a puppy. From the first, he was attracted to the footplate rather than the carriages, but as the years went by and his tastes matured he did sometimes ride in more comfort than the driver and fireman could provide. He was much loved by all the railway staff simply because he was so friendly. He would sit quietly by the driver and somehow never manage to impede his work or that of the numerous firemen who knew and loved him.

Jock regarded the Scottish Central Railway as his own particular railway, and Perth as his principal place of residence, but he made frequent trips to Aberdeen, Edinburgh, York and London. When he arrived at Perth station in the mornings – and he arrived ready to travel as often as three or four times per week – the staff simply patted him and let him through without a ticket. He would then simply choose whichever train took his fancy, climb aboard and wait for the off.

When he became really well known, drivers and firemen would be stricken at the sight of Jock climbing aboard someone else's train. On several occasions he got as far as Paris, where a Perth businessman recognised his familiar face. Three days later the businessman was in Lyon and there, resting on the main platform, was Jock.

Wherever he went, Jock always returned within a week or ten days to Perth, but he was generally happy travelling each day with other commuters to Glasgow or Edinburgh. Once he travelled to London and vanished for nearly three weeks. Among the drivers and firemen there was talk of little else. Then a railway official spotted Jock in a rough-looking pet shop near King's Cross station in London. The official protested to the shop owner, who insisted he had come by Jock legitimately. There was nothing for it and the railway official bought Jock and only released him when they reached the station. As soon as he was let down on the platform, Jock ran about in an ecstasy of tail-wagging and happy yelping. As soon as the Edinburgh express arrived, he was greeted with cheers and pats by the crew before leaping aboard for the first part of his journey home.

When he died, the whole of the Scottish Central Railway went into mourning. It was estimated that his regular appearances around the station and his friendliness to everyone had actually made the Scottish Central Railway a more prosperous railway company than it would have been without Jock. It was even said that people booked their tickets partly to get where they wanted to go and partly to meet up with their old friend Jock once again. No one claimed the little body when it was found that he'd died quietly in his sleep, and his passion for railways was never explained – all we know is that railways were the love of his life.

TRIAL BY FIRE

AMERICA, 1892

The great difference between train journeys in the United States and train journeys in the UK can be summed up in one word: distance. And of course, when the Wild West was first opened up at the end of the nineteenth century, the railway engineers had to cope with difficult terrain, angry Native Americans, outlaws and a huge territory that had only minimal policing and infrastructure.

This led to a situation in which, at times, and on certain journeys, there was only a fifty-fifty chance that you would reach your destination unscathed. If the train wasn't attacked by native tribes, the tracks might have been ripped up by angry settlers or washed away by flood and tempest.

Among the more unusual hazards to which rail travellers were once subjected was fire. On one journey through the Midwest in the 1890s, for more than 100 miles (161km), the train had to run through a prairie that was on fire from horizon to horizon. For the nearly three hours it took to pass through the flames the passengers were asked to wear blankets previously soaked in water. They were also asked to keep looking out the windows in case the paint on the sides of the carriages began to blister or even burst into flame. When this happened, buckets of water were passed down the corridors and tipped out the window over the fire, wherever it happened to be. In this way, the train managed to get through the burning prairie without mishap. The only difficulty was that the passengers were exhausted and covered in wet soot by the time they arrived at their destination. But then, as one man was heard to comment: 'It wasn't near damn as dangerous as travelling out west in the old stage-coach days!'

CLAIMS FOR DAMAGES

ENGLAND, 1892

It wasn't long after railway travel became widely available that the railway companies realised that they would need to be insured if they were to survive claims for damages following accidents. With the best will in the world, they knew that however many safety precautions were put in place, accidents were bound still to happen now and then and, without insurance, the claims of injured passengers could easily put a company out of business. But word quickly spread that injured passengers were receiving substantial sums of money and numerous fraudulent claims were uncovered over the years. On at least one occasion, a man sitting on a railway embankment spotted a derailment half a mile away (0.8km) and immediately ran to the scene of the accident. He rolled around in the spilled oil and dirt, tore his clothes and knocked his head against a few twisted pieces of metal. He later made a claim against the railway company and received more than £100 in compensation – a considerable sum in the 1870s. He was only found out when a policeman overheard him boasting about his new-found wealth in a local pub.

The most extraordinary example of a false claim for an accident concerned a woman who travelled regularly in the 1890s in the Southern Region. She sued the railway company for injuries sustained when she slipped on the platform while running for a train.

When the case came to court, a railway official thought the woman looked rather familiar and, through the railway's lawyers, he managed to get the judge to give him more time to conduct investigations. After some skilful detective work, he established that this was the fourth accident for which the company had been asked to pay this particular woman, and on the last occasion she had been awarded a very large sum of money as a result of total and permanent paralysis!

When the judge heard the new evidence, he dismissed the case and warned the woman never again to waste the court's time or she might well end up behind bars.

JUST A QUICK ONE
ENGLAND, 1894

It took nearly three years before regular commuters on all the main lines out of London – to the north-east, north-west, south, south-east and south-west – became aware of something slightly odd. When the rumours spread and an investigation had been set up by the railway companies, the pieces quickly came together, and it was established that the bizarre confidence trick had begun two and a half years earlier on commuter trains leaving Euston in the evenings.

Just as the train was about to leave, a well-spoken young man was seen running along the platform shouting up at passengers through the open windows.

'A woman has fainted – does anyone have any brandy or whisky?'

Invariably – this being the 1890s – someone would have a hip flask and it would be handed down.

'That's terribly kind. I'll just go and administer a dose and be right back.'

The young man dashed back along the platform like some latter-day Sir Galahad. But the elderly gentleman who'd handed over his hip flask waited in vain for it to be returned. He spoke to the guard and the ticket collector. Neither knew a thing about a woman fainting.

It was assumed that this, the first victim of the hip-flask trickster as he became known, was not a victim at all. The ticket collector reassured the elderly passenger that in the rush to bring help to a woman in distress his hip flask had probably not been returned simply because the woman had to be taken off the train and the young man had accompanied her.

Over the coming months the same or a similar trick was carried out on trains about to leave King's Cross, Liverpool Street, Victoria and Waterloo. The young man escaped detection because he carried out his little deception only once every two weeks and each time at a different station. But then he became overconfident and his hit rate increased to once, sometimes twice a week.

He was finally arrested when a passenger remembered a similar earlier incident. The passenger reported his suspicions to the guard, who collared the young man as he headed towards the station entrance. The police later found 30 silver flasks at the young man's home, but it was suspected that he'd already sold on many more.

JUSTICE BY RAIL
WALES, 1898

Today, businesspeople regularly work on the train as they travel to and from work or on longer journeys around the country or even around the world. The fact that work is possible while travelling has always made the train an attractive option compared with, say, the car. But work of a far wider variety once took place on many railway journeys. One of the strangest examples occurred in South Wales, where a carriage was turned into an official law court.

It all began when Judge Williams, who had been trying a case in Bridgend County Court, found that he could not finish it on the same day. One important witness had still to be examined. The judge knew he could not continue the following morning because he was due at another court first thing next day and the other court was many miles away.

Determined not to put the parties to the case to the expense of what would have proved a lengthy adjournment, the judge suggested a plan to the barristers involved and then rushed off to the station, where he was joined in the carriage by the lawyers, the defendant (suitably accompanied) and the important witness.

As the train pursued its journey, the witness gave his evidence and was cross-examined at some length by both barristers. Instead of adjourning for lunch, the 'court' simply waited until the train reached a station with a decent cafe and then dashed in for a sandwich and tea. A barrister sat between the judge and the defendant over lunch, but later remarked that he found the whole proceeding far more enjoyable and conducive to justice than the stuffy confines of the traditional courtroom restaurant.

When the train reached its destination, the whole party alighted and set off for the stationmaster's office, where the judge delivered his verdict.

BIG WOMAN
CANADA, 1898

Certain railway jobs have always attracted men of a thoughtful cast of mind. The signalman's trade is a good example. Many signal boxes were in extremely remote places where there might only be a few trains each day. In between trains, as it were, the signalman had time to think. Many were great readers; others kept detailed accounts of all they saw around them, at least one mended clocks and another built a canoe.

Porters, drivers and firemen inevitably had less time to record what was going on but at least one booking-office clerk – a Canadian – wrote a regular column for his local newspaper about the odd characters he and his fellow booking-office clerks came across now and then in the line of duty.

His favourite tale, which was recorded by him in 1898, concerned what he rather unkindly referred to as 'a vigorous lady of the elephantine type'.

She appeared at the ticket gate of a Canadian Pacific Railway station and asked for a ticket to Vankleek Hill.

The booking-office clerk on duty that day – not the recorder of the tale – was a thin, pallid-faced man. When the rather large woman asked for her ticket the clerk enquired laconically: 'Single?'

With a look of withering scorn and resentment the woman replied: 'It ain't none of your business whether I'm single, married or a widder. I might have been married a dozen times or more if I had felt like providing for a lazy, shiftless, good-fer-nothin' shrivelled-up bit of a man like you!'

He sold her a single.

GHOULISH PASSENGER

ENGLAND, 1898

One of the greatest difficulties with railway travel is that one cannot easily choose one's companions. Most travellers, of course, fit well within the broad range of what might be described as fairly ordinary and we therefore barely notice them when we share a carriage; those few who seem a little more eccentric or outlandish or even threatening than the norm represent a far smaller group, but these are the people we remember.

Today, when most trains have open-plan carriages with perhaps 50 or more people seated in them, the influence of eccentric characters is somewhat diluted, but, in the days when carriages were made up of small compartments got up pretty much like the old stage-coaches, things were very different.

A Sussex newspaper reported in the 1890s the experience of a young but rather timid mother who entered a compartment on the early morning train from Brighton to London. She had made herself and her child comfortable by the window and, hearing the whistle that indicated the train's imminent departure, was looking forward to having the carriage to herself, when a tall and very gloomy individual entered her compartment and shut the door. He sat down and stared fixedly ahead. She later described his complexion as white to the point of death and explained how her discomfort increased dramatically when, to her cheerful 'Good morning', he returned only a mournful stare.

She decided that a journey to London with such a man almost opposite her was more than she could endure, but she was reluctant to move to another compartment after feeling so pleased with herself at having discovered this one empty. But how could she get rid of him? Then, just as she was about to give up and move, she had an idea: she decided to be courageous and tell a white lie.

She leaned across to her fellow traveller and said in a loud and determined voice: 'I just thought I ought to tell you that my little girl here has only just recovered from a dreadful attack of scarlet fever and I fear she is still highly infectious.'

'Oh don't worry about me, mum,' interrupted the man, 'I'm committing suicide when we get to the first tunnel.'

The horrified woman packed her things, clutched her child to her bosom and changed compartments. The next passenger who joined the gloomy man might have noticed that he had cheered up no end. Needless to say, he did not commit suicide when the train reached the first tunnel.

LANGUAGE DIFFICULTIES
INDIA, 1899

A tea planter and his family were late arriving at the station for the train that was to take them away from the stifling heat of summer in Bombay to the cool of the north and the slopes of the Himalayas. The Raj was still unquestioned at this time and of course Europeans were always treated as a cut above the rest, so the family – a father and his two daughters – was allowed to board the train without buying their tickets.

However, the tea planter's confident assertion that the family would pay at the other end of their journey was taken with a pinch of salt by the booking-office clerk. Like all good Indian bureaucrats, he did things by the book, and as soon as the train carrying the family north had steamed out of the station he wired ahead to the booking office at the other end of the line.

His telegraph message, which became famous throughout the Indian Railway Service, ran as follows: 'Obtain fares. Three Europeans travelling first class sleeping compartment in night attire. One adult and two adultresses.'

BLOCKING THE TRACKS
AMERICA, 1900

At one stage in the nineteenth century, American railroad companies employed so many conductors that passengers' tickets were clipped, stamped and punched, it seemed, every few miles. This overmanning developed gradually in response to the railroad owners' almost obsessive desire to catch all those who travelled without buying a ticket. Soon the costs of preventing fraud, largely the costs of extra ticket inspectors, hugely outweighed the benefits – it just wasn't worth it and by the time the railroad company realised their mistake there were an awful lot of people to be got rid of. No one likes to lose their job, but railroad staff who'd expected a job for life were in some cases very angry indeed when they discovered they were to be laid off.

One conductor was so furious that he paid a group of his friends to block the track with a pile of old sleepers. It was on a section where the train didn't travel so fast that there were likely to be many fatalities, but, when the engine and three carriages came off the track, the conductor – who was on the very train he'd deliberately sabotaged – refused to help in any way. He sat on a rock nearby and when asked why he didn't do his duty and try to restore some order to the chaos he merely replied: 'They damn well laid me off, I want to see how they like it now! They want to do without me? Now they can damn well do without me!'

WICKED TONGUE

ENGLAND, 1900

The guard on a train was once vitally important. He literally guarded the train and its passengers while the driver got on with the more straightforward business of keeping the thing moving. Until relatively recently, guards used a hand brake to assist the vacuum brakes applied by the driver and they kept an eye on the passengers and carriages to see that there were no problems.

Guards tended to be a law unto themselves and they would take no nonsense from other railway employees, whether they be drivers, managers or even at times directors.

A famously bad-tempered guard on the Great Northern Railway became something of a legend: he'd been known to box the ears of cheeky boys, he would intervene if he felt young ladies were reading unsuitable magazines or novels and on several occasions he found someone smoking in a non-smoking compartment and put them off the train at the next station. He once ejected a foreign diplomat for this offence and, when the spluttering and indignant smoker threatened to contact the guard's superiors, the guard shouted back, 'I ain't got any superiors!'

But this guard of the old school could also be charming and amusing. He was much loved by regular passengers, who enjoyed listening to him sing famous operatic arias, and he was a famous wit. Perhaps his greatest sally came when he found a passenger leaning out of the window.

'Put your head inside, sir,' he shouted to the passenger as the train steamed out of the station.

'I shall do as I like,' retorted the passenger.

'All right,' came the reply. 'Do as you please, but you must understand that you'll be held liable for all damage done to the stonework of the company's bridges.'

ANOTHER
EXTRAORDINARY ESCAPE
ENGLAND, 1903

Many hair's-breadth escapes from almost certain death have been recorded in the annals of railway history, one of the most wonderful being that of the man who, in the early days of corridor trains, stepped out on the wrong side of a Great Western express running at 60mph (96.6km/h), and alighted on the tracks without receiving a scratch.

Passengers unused to the idea of corridors often mistakenly chose the wrong side of a compartment, particularly if it was late at night or they'd had a few drinks – in fact, the railway companies became so worried that, for a while, on some trains they put up signs saying 'Corridor this way!'

Almost more marvellous than the man who hit the tracks at 60mph and lived to tell the tale was the case of Messrs Hussey (father and son) who, while crossing the line at Round Oak station, on 14 March 1903, were run over by an engine and van. Witnesses said later that the two men were right in the path of the engine when they were hit and should not have survived, since even a glancing blow from an engine would be enough in most cases to cause instant death.

In this case the engine was fitted with a water scoop, which left less than 1 foot (30.5cm) between it and the ground, and yet the two men were practically unhurt, and travelled by the train for which they had booked. The incidents of their arrival at the station, hair's-breadth escape and departure by train were crowded into the space of a few minutes.

PHILANTHROPIST ON THE TRAIN

ENGLAND, 1903

From the very beginning, trains have exerted a strange pull on a certain percentage of the population. This percentage is almost exclusively male and highly prone to making lists. We don't know when the earliest trainspotters appeared on the scene, but it's certain that within a few years of railway services being established young men and old became fascinated by them. For most, this fascination took the form of recording sightings of particular trains or learning everything there was to know about how engines were made and routes established. But one remarkable man found trains so compelling that they made him give a great deal of his money away. It all began innocently enough. An elderly woman travelling on the Great Western Region for her annual holiday in Cornwall was approached by the ticket collector and told that she'd been invited to dine in the first-class dining carriage. When she protested that she was quite happy to eat her sandwiches, the guard explained that an elderly gentleman would be enormously grateful if she would have lunch at his expense. Unable to resist the temptation, she enjoyed what she later described as the best meal of her life. But, when she approached the ticket collector and asked if she might meet and thank her benefactor, he explained that the elderly gentleman was virtually a recluse and found meeting new people extremely difficult.

Similar incidents occurred pretty frequently over the coming months and the story reached the local newspapers. Who on earth was this elderly eccentric who kept buying other elderly people expensive lunches? No one knew. Then there was a further development. Ticket collectors reported being asked to offer passengers cash and cheques – not for huge sums but enough to make a real difference. In each case the recipient appeared down on his or her luck and in each case the intermediary was a ticket collector. The wealthy reclusive train traveller would never meet those to whom he gave, but he did pass on the same message each time he made a donation. He would always say – and each time through the ticket collector – 'I hope you have enjoyed your journey and that this money will persuade you again in the future to travel on the greatest transport invention ever made.'

It was only when a startled beneficiary was asked to describe which ticket collector had passed on the message and the cheque that railway officials realised what had been happening. The ticket collector was described as stout and red-faced with a thick head of white hair. It just happened that the ticket collector on this particular train was one of the best known on the GWR, and he bore absolutely no relation to the description. The eccentric philanthropist had been impersonating a ticket collector, but after the story appeared in the local newspapers the phantom ticket collector was never seen or heard of again. His identity was never discovered.

DREAMING DRIVER

AMERICA, 1903

A well-known American engine driver with 25 years' experience claimed to have premonitions of incidents in which his locomotive was overturned or derailed. Each time he had dreamed beforehand of the accident, seeing in the dream the exact place, the direction in which the train was going and the side on which the engine was overturned.

At various times his dreams came early enough and with sufficient detail to prevent collisions; over a number of years local newspapers credited him with saving many lives and much property in this way.

He recorded one of his extraordinary experiences in a specially written feature for a long-forgotten newspaper.

At one time I was in charge of a construction train, being driver, conductor and gang-boss combined. One night I saw in a dream the collision of an express with a through freight train at the station where I stopped. The engines and coaches were badly smashed up and many killed and wounded. The dream was very vivid and distressed me all the next day. The second morning my train was ready to start, but the through freight, which was late, came along, passing the station within seven minutes of the express train, a very reckless thing, as it was in a cutting which had a sharp curve, through which the express always came at full speed. At that very moment, to my horror I heard the whistle of the express. It recalled my dream at once.

Seizing the red flag, I signalled the freight train, and ran down the curve to flag the express, whose driver reversed at once, and the engines came to a halt within 10ft (3m) of each other.

As it was not my duty to flag other trains, or to pay any attention to them, had it not been for the dream and its effects on my mind, causing me to be doubly on the alert at that time, there would have been a serious collision, as the express had nine very full coaches. Some considered it a lucky coincidence, but these, in my experience, have been too frequent, and the dreams too real for me to consider them as such.

MOBBED BY MAGPIES

RUSSIA AND CHINA, 1903

Oliver Ready travelled through Siberia and Manchuria (now in China) by rail in 1903. His account of the journey is filled with fascinating details. When the train, leaving Germany and entering Russia, stopped at the border town of Alexandrowo, for example, the Russian officials stood at one end of the platform staring malevolently at the German officials at the other. Neither side would speak to the other. The Russians wore white smocks down to the ground, the Germans stiff, uncomfortable uniforms of the Kaiser's army. At the railway hotel in Warsaw, Ready could hardly eat his dinner because the dining room was so bright. An official later told him it was lit by more than a thousand gas lights.

The trans-Siberian railway was hugely overcrowded throughout its long journey, and passports were demanded all hours of the day and night – sometimes as often as a dozen times in one night. Despite having a first-class ticket, Ready had to sleep on top of the huge piles of luggage that littered every surface area – carriage floors, seats and beds. In a compartment designed for two, he found nine people sleeping.

During the 5,000-mile (8,047km) journey, Ready met a most remarkable man. He had never left his small Siberian village, yet his English was perfect and he was a huge fan of Jane Austen and of Hampshire's chalkstream trout fishing!

For two days Ready listened to an extraordinary stream of anecdotes, first about *Emma* or *Pride and Prejudice*, then about the best dry fly for the Itchen or Test at certain times of year.

The rather one-sided conversation only came to an end when they reached a station at which a vast volley of gunfire was heard. Ready stuck his head out of a window and discovered several hundred soldiers lined up along the platform firing continually into the air. No one seemed to know why. And at the next station, where the train waited for several hours, a group of bedraggled men, women and children were marched behind a wall at gunpoint by a group of soldiers. This was followed by the sound of shooting and then the soldiers reappeared but without the group of civilians. Ready was terribly shocked, but the other passengers merely shrugged.

As Ready's extraordinary journey reached its end, the train was mobbed by thousands of magpies, and for the last 100 miles (161km), there was an armed Chinese guard stationed every 100 yards (91.4m) by the side of the tracks.

A MAN IN A DRESS
FRANCE, 1905

Before the Great War, passports were hardly necessary, at least in Europe. Those few wealthy individuals who could afford to travel simply got on a boat and got off on the other side of the Channel or the North Sea. Customs officials might harass them over wine or tobacco duties, but that was about it. The fact that the vast majority of Europeans never travelled anywhere can be attributed to the fact that the travel industry and the low-cost travel it made possible did not yet exist.

This lack of interchange between countries also meant, of course, that we knew less about each other's cultures than we do now. Most villagers had never left the place where they were born and grew up, which meant, for example, that in remote rural parts of Greece the national costume was at least in part still worn and men looked pretty much like Elizabethan courtiers in their doublet and hose. Television and the ubiquitous use of English had yet to make them realise that the rest of the world was not as they were.

The lack of awareness of other people's cultures led occasionally to embarrassment, hilarity or both, as a gentleman from Scotland discovered while travelling through rural France by train. He had travelled down from his native Edinburgh with no problems, for Queen Victoria had made all things Scottish highly fashionable, and our traveller believed that the habits and dress of Scotland should be better known right across Europe. He had therefore donned kilt, sporran and dirk before setting out on his long train journey to the South of France.

Having crossed the Channel, all went well. He slept till he reached Paris, changed trains and continued on his way. He did arouse astonishment in Paris but it was kept within bounds and amounted to little more than a bit of pointing and a few open mouths. But, as the train for the south travelled through the more rustic regions of rural France, this situation changed. At last the train stopped at a remote station and two elderly, respectable and highly religious ladies entered the Scotsman's carriage. At first all went well, for the Scotsman was asleep under a blanket. But at last he woke and stood up to leave the carriage in order to stretch his legs in the corridor. At once the two elderly Frenchwomen began to scream and shout. The Scotsman stood dumbfounded until the guard, breathless in his haste, entered the compartment. The two women, still in an almost hysterical rage, demanded the removal of the pervert in petticoats. The guard, who knew a great deal about the world and had travelled widely for his job, pointed out that the Scotsman was simply dressed in the costume of his country.

The Frenchwomen were unmoved. 'To ride with a man in a dress!' They almost spat the words. 'It is impossible, *incroyable*, it is not proper, not even decent.' They told the guard that unless something was done they would pull the communication cord the instant the train left the station. There was nothing for it. The guard helped the two women carry their luggage to a first-class compartment and the look of satisfaction on their faces when they arrived at their new seats seemed somehow not entirely attributable to their escape from the man in petticoats.

RAILWAY WIT
ENGLAND, 1906

Railway staff were famous at one time for their sardonic wit. This probably had to do with the fact that they were constantly dealing with a largely indifferent or ungrateful public. But the public ultimately paid their wages, and senior staff would not tolerate sharp words to the travelling public, even when the travelling public probably deserved it.

The only way round the problem was to learn to respond in ways that enabled the staff to let off steam while leaving the public unsure whether they had been ticked off or not.

Wit was also a vital tool for relationships between staff and, as in many jobs and professions, railway people had countless 'in-jokes' and sayings that outsiders would have found baffling. Among the legendary conversations retold endlessly was the one between a stationmaster, a customer – in this case the customer had sent a parcel by rail – a porter and a booking clerk.

The stationmaster was famous for tolerating no other opinion than his own, and was therefore always right. Early one morning he found himself in the thick of a dispute about why and how exactly a parcel sent by train had been damaged. The sender declared that the breakages were due to the carelessness of the porter handling them, while the porter was highly indignant at the suggestion and called attention to the fact that the box was badly packed.

'I expect, if the truth's known,' said the booking clerk, putting in his oar, 'it was six of one and half a dozen of the other.'

'You weren't asked for your opinion, Mr Jenkins,' snapped the stationmaster irritably. 'And, as it happens, you're quite wrong – it was just the opposite.'

But real wit among railwaymen could come from the youngest members of staff, as a little snippet from an East London local paper of the Edwardian era reveals. The railway company had been taking on new van boys at the goods depot, and among the applicants was a smart little Cockney lad. The little lad reached the front of the queue and was interviewed by the gaffer.

'What's your name?' asked the gaffer.

''Arry Coggins, sir.'

'Where do you live?' came the next query.

'Lambeth, sir.'

'Lambeth, eh? Have you lived there all your life?'

'No, not yet, sir,' came the prompt retort.

WHISKY BARREL

SCOTLAND, 1906

Life is always difficult for the churchman who likes to drink. In the Anglican and Catholic churches drinking in moderation is just about tolerated, but among the stricter Protestant sects, particularly the Presbyterians, the very idea of drink is anathema. Which creates the curious paradox that the country that produces some of the most delicious alcoholic drink in the world – namely Scotland – also produces some of the strictest Presbyterians.

Occasionally drink and Presbyterianism do battle, and drink is invariably the winner. A classic case occurred when the stationmaster at Mallaig spoke to the purser of the West Highland steamer, which had just berthed after a journey from the Isle of Lewis – an island famous for putting padlocks on the children's swings to prevent fun on the Sabbath.

The stationmaster shouted to the purser: 'Any goods for the Glasgow train?'

'Aye,' came the answer. 'Two jars of whisky.'

But having been told to expect whisky, the stationmaster was astonished to see a large flour barrel and an earthenware jar swung aboard the train.

'But that's not a whisky jar!' he shouted.

'Oh don't worry yersel,' came the reply. 'The jar is for the Established Church minister. The other – the flour barrel – has a whisky jar hidden in it for the Free Kirk minister!'

MR LEAROYD'S RECORD
ENGLAND, 1910

A whim for attempting novel things and a penchant for touring led Mr J. Ingham Learoyd, a well-known Halifax businessman, to test the possibility of travelling 1,000 miles (1,610km) on a British railway in a single day. His first plan was to attempt the feat by zigzagging across, but the timetables made this impossible and the idea of hiring special trains was dismissed on the grounds of expense. The only way to do it – despite the bizarre pointlessness of the proceeding – was to travel long distances to and fro on one system. Mr Ingham Learoyd chose the Midland.

Starting from London's St Pancras station at midnight one Monday, Mr Learoyd journeyed to Leeds, reaching that city at 4.03am. In seven minutes he began the return journey, getting back to St Pancras at 8.15am, having so far accounted for 391½ miles (630km) in 488 minutes. Next, after boarding the 9.30am North Express again at St Pancras, he was rushed to Carlisle, some 308½ miles (496km) away, arriving there at 3.50pm, or in 380 minutes, and leaving only an eight-minute margin before he had to be seated in a return train for London, due at 10.25pm.

Punctuality was so assured in those far-off days that the entire programme, fine as the margins were, was carried through as planned: 1,008 miles (1,622km) were travelled in, as nearly as possible, 1,260 minutes, or 180 minutes inside the specified time. Mr Learoyd carried a certificate with three of his portraits for identification purposes and, at each terminal by pre-arrangement, a railway official stamped specially prepared documentation.

The intrepid traveller said that for two years he had been contemplating his strange journey, and that during that time he had studied the timetables so intensively that he knew them off by heart. Learoyd actually spent just 21 hours travelling, and the distance he covered worked out at an average of 48mph (77.2km/h).

SLIGHT MISUNDERSTANDING

ENGLAND, 1911

A bishop spent an hour trying to locate the stationmaster at Paddington in order to have a porter sacked. The bishop was furious because he thought the porter had deliberately insulted him. It was only when the circumstances had been explained to the stationmaster that the bishop – famously tetchy and convinced of his own importance – realised that he had made a complete fool of himself.

The story begins with the system for dealing with luggage at Paddington. In the early days it was the practice for luggage coming by train to be carried to a long bench overhung by the letters of the alphabet. To claim his luggage Mr Smith would, for example, go to the letter S, Mr Brown to the letter B and so on.

When the bishop, a little the worse for drink, arrived at the station he found a porter and – completely ignorant of the Paddington method for sorting luggage – asked where he should go to find his bags.

'What is your name?' said the porter.

'Llewellyn,' said the bishop.

'Go to L,' said the porter.

The bishop's face turned red and without a word he set off in search of the stationmaster.

SIGNING THE PEACE
FRANCE, 1918

Over the past 150 years and more, children have no doubt occasionally been conceived in railway carriages. Women have given birth on trains and, sadly, the elderly have been known to depart this world while on a journey on the iron road. Many other momentous events have taken place on trains, from murders to christenings, seances to marriages. But perhaps the most momentous event ever recorded in a railway carriage occurred in 1918.

A replica of the carriage now stands on a sector of what was the Western Front during the First World War. Long removed from active service, the carriage is, in appearance, just an ordinary carriage, typical of the design used by the French Railway Service in the years up to and after the Great War, but within it was signed the Armistice that stilled the millions of guns and rifles that for more than four years had levied their toll of death over a 1,000-mile (1.610km) front.

Few places have the significance of this simple carriage, where the document was signed that brought peace to a grief-stricken Europe.

TRAIN ROBBERS MEET THEIR MATCH

ENGLAND, 1925

One would think that strange rail journeys would be exclusively associated with drivers, guards and passengers, and not with the signalman in his often lonely and isolated box. But of course there are exceptions to every rule, and at least one signalman got mixed up in a remarkable adventure.

It all began when the railway authorities got wind of a plan to hold up and rob a train that was conveying boxes of gold to Southampton for shipment to America. The secret of the shipment had somehow leaked out, and half a dozen desperate characters, ex-jailbirds, apparently decided that the gold had better stay in England and with them.

The first part of their plan to steal the gold involved overpowering an elderly signalman at a lonely countryside place, afterwards working the signals themselves. They proposed to bring the gold train to a standstill, tie up the driver and the guard, and carry away the spoils by car.

Perhaps the plan was inspired by something the criminals had seen at the cinema. They thought their plan was foolproof, but then fate took a hand in events. The old signalman was taken ill with a serious bout of flu and a younger man came to do the job for a time. He was a strong man, too, and an amateur boxer who could have been a professional but for the fact that he loved his job on the railways. When the train robbers climbed the steps of his box in the dead of night, little did they suspect what awaited them.

The first robber crept through the door, made a rush at the signalman in the half-light and was knocked clean unconscious by a perfectly executed right hook. The signalman reached the door of his box and the next man came at him up the stairs. Train robber number two was knocked flying. From then on the signalman knocked them down the steps of the signal box as fast as they came up, and the gold train ran by in safety while they were counting their bruises. Afterwards the police rounded up the lot of them and, covered as they were in fresh cuts and bruises, there were few problems identifying them!

HOPELESS VOLUNTEER
ENGLAND, 1926

During the General Strike, volunteer firemen, drivers, porters and guards were taken on, and in general they made a thoroughly bad job of running those industries that had come to a halt as the result of the walkout. On the railway most of the volunteers were from well-off backgrounds and had no experience of hard manual work of any kind. Many were lucky enough to have private incomes as they were, to be frank, fit for no kind of employment. The railway was particularly badly afflicted with this kind of volunteer, but their presence led to one or two amusing incidents. A good example occurred on a suburban train that left London and then had a long steep climb. It made it to the top of the incline by the narrowest of margins and the volunteer guard ran to the front of the train to discuss their narrow escape with the driver.

'My word,' said the driver, as the volunteer guard reached the footplate, 'I never thought we'd make the top of that hill.'

'Yes,' said the volunteer guard, 'and you have me to thank for the fact that we didn't run backwards. Thank goodness I screwed the brake down hard!'

STRANGE PACKAGE

ENGLAND, 1926

The officers of the Midland Railway depot in Liverpool were asked to go down to the platform where a strange package from the South of France had just arrived on the 8.35 express. The package was destined to be sent on to the USA, but there was something highly suspicious about it. The guard on the train had raised the alarm after noticing a strange smell.

The increasingly large group of railway officials had the package, which was rather large, carried to the railway post office. There they debated whether or not they should open it. Under normal circumstances any package entrusted to the railway was treated with the utmost discretion, and opening a packet without permission was something contemplated only in extreme circumstances. But the longer they looked at the package, the more worried they became. A decision was made to open the crate. When this was done it was found to contain a beautifully ornamented coffin containing the embalmed body of an American, fully dressed and complete with cowboy hat, guns, belt and boots.

Under the rules of parcel-carrying that existed in the nineteenth century, bodies were not permitted to be posted around the world. There was nothing for it but to impound the coffin and its cowboy. The crate was sealed up again and left in the lost property office, while officials contacted the Chicago station that was its destination. In Chicago, advertisements were taken out to try to trace the owners of the crate, but two years later no one had come forward and the embalmed cowboy's identity remained a mystery.

After that, all efforts to trace the owners of the crate or relatives of the dead American ceased, and the crate remained at Liverpool for more than 20 years. Most of those who'd stood around examining the coffin when it was first discovered were long dead or retired by the time an official checking the old ledgers spotted an entry for the coffin and noted too that the crate had never been collected. He took down the reference number that indicated where the crate was stored but, when he went to check it was still there, not a trace could be found. And it has not been seen since.

MYSTERY CHILDREN

ENGLAND, 1928

Early one misty October morning, a Bristol-bound freight train, a passenger train from Birmingham and an empty 50-wagon train collided near the village of Charfield, at that time still in Gloucestershire. Several people were killed, including two children. A terrible tragedy by any standards, but also the beginning of one of the greatest unsolved mysteries, for the two children who died have never been identified.

The railway company insisted the two children had not been on the train and that the two small bodies actually belonged to two strays who'd been sheltering under the railway bridge at the time of the crash. But the driver of the passenger train survived the crash and spoke up. He explained how he had waved to the two well-dressed children when they boarded the train at New Street, Birmingham. He had noticed them – the girl aged about eight, the boy eleven – because they were unaccompanied and without luggage.

Legend has it that for years after the crash an elderly woman in black, driven by a chauffeur, visited the grave at Charfield where ten victims of the crash (including the children) are buried. After the war, she ceased to come, and there is no evidence anyway that her visits were not to remember one of the other victims. As each year passes there is less chance of identifying the children and their story remains one of the greatest of all railway mysteries.

MISSING MUMMY

ENGLAND, 1930

It's almost impossible to believe now but in the late nineteenth century tens of thousands of mummified cats and other mummified animals plundered from Egyptian tombs were shipped by train and boat to Liverpool, ground down and then sold to farmers in the north-west of England to be used as fertiliser.

But with the discovery of Tutankhamen's tomb in 1922, Egyptology was suddenly taken far more seriously. The quality of the artefacts discovered was extraordinary, and their design had an enormous influence on culture and art generally and more specifically on the Art Deco movement of the 1920s and 1930s. Mummies – at least of humans – suddenly became valuable commodities, and they were transported from the Valley of the Kings to museums and collectors all over the world. Anyone with any pretensions to wealth and taste wanted a mummy in their art collection, which meant prices soared and the black market trade flourished.

One particularly interesting and valuable mummy was discovered in Egypt and sold to a wealthy collector in the North of England. It consisted of a beautifully carved stone sarcophagus containing a magnificently decorated wooden casket and, inside that, the mummified remains of a princess. Every inch of the wooden casket was covered with hieroglyphics; the portrait of the deceased on the head of the casket was particularly fine, and the bandages that enclosed the mummy were still decorated with the beads and other pieces of jewellery that had lain undisturbed for more than 3,000 years.

But how was this priceless antiquity to be brought safely to Cheshire? The answer was first by rail to the port of Alexandria and then by ship to Liverpool. From there the train would have to carry the princess to the grand house in Cheshire that was to be her new home.

All went well on the first two stages of the journey, and it was only when the North Western Railway Company took charge that things began to go wrong. In its big wooden crate, the stone sarcophagus and its contents weighed several tons, and when the time came for it to be loaded into the train on the docks, it took more than a dozen porters to manoeuvre the thing into the specially commissioned freight wagon in which it was to be transported. All went well and the train was soon speeding away from the smoky city out into the countryside.

By the time the train had stopped at the first of three scheduled stops, something quite extraordinary had happened. The freight wagon was no longer attached to the train – it had vanished. No one had seen it go, and enquiries up and down the line over the next few days revealed absolutely nothing about its whereabouts. There were two single branch lines it could have taken – though how anyone could have removed it from the train, changed the points and manoeuvred the wagon off down a different line baffled police and railway investigators.

Months passed and nothing was heard of the mummy. Then eight months after the incident, a schoolboy playing in fields at the edge of one of the branch lines discovered the badly damaged freight wagon. It had been cleverly concealed under masses of brushwood, leaves and branches in thick woodland at the bottom of the railway embankment. All traces of its derailment from the line above and down through the trees had been obliterated. The point on the line where the wagon had been deliberately derailed was just a few hundred yards from the junction with the main line and, once it had been discovered, it seemed extraordinary that it hadn't been spotted before.

This was all long before police work had the benefit of forensic science, so the examination of the freight wagon and surrounding area was at best cursory. Nothing of any significance was found but one thing was clear – the valuable mummy, its casket and the sarcophagus were long gone. But how on earth had such a large, heavy object been carried across the field, presumably to the nearest road, and then carted away without anything being seen?

Over the next two years, the mummy's owner received reports that it had been spotted in various museums around the world but, when he made enquiries, it always turned out to be a different mummy. Trying to track down his lost mummy became something of a crusade for the wealthy aristocrat. He spent a great deal of money on private detectives who travelled Europe checking museums and private collections. He took to travelling the country – by train, of course – and hung around left luggage offices in the vain hope that his long-lost prize possession would somehow materialise. It never did and the old man died without ever recovering his property.

In a curious twist there were reports 20 years after the old man died that a stone coffin covered with strange writing was found half buried in a field 200 miles (322km) from the place where the mummy originally disappeared. In a curious twist of fate, the stone coffin was found just a few yards from a railway line, but, by the time anyone realised that it was a thing of some value, it had been broken up by workmen and dispersed.

FAITHFUL SERVANT
ENGLAND, 1930

In June 1930, Tom Holton's father was stationmaster at Towcester and the family lived in the station house. When Tom's sister died in an epidemic, the railway company put on a special train to carry the coffin and mourners to their ancestral home at the village of Slapton, 5 miles (8km) away.

The train waited at the nearest point to the church while bearers carried the coffin half a mile (0.8km) along a field path to the churchyard where the burial took place. The track was a single line so no other train could pass. The family were then conveyed back to Towcester.

The train company, the Stratford-upon-Avon and Midland Junction Railway, was more than once in the receiver's hands, but it was not too poor to pay this compliment to a faithful servant.

STOP THE TRAIN

SCOTLAND, 1935

The North of Scotland Railway runs through some of Europe's most remote countryside. But, despite the remoteness of the countryside, the enthusiastic railway builders had allowed for a station wherever they thought there might be the least interest in occasional travel. This meant there were lots of stations in the middle of nowhere.

To reduce the huge costs of stopping the trains at these outposts regularly, a rule was established that the trains would slow down as they ran through the stations and stop only if a passenger was there on the platform and trying to flag the train down. This worked well in most areas, but one or two of the older farmers didn't quite grasp the principle of the thing, and for years railway staff dined out on the story of old McMurdo, who flagged down one of the few busy trains early one evening. The engine driver knew McMurdo and was astonished to see him waving the train down – McMurdo was famous for never travelling anywhere whatever the circumstances.

But he was certainly waving, and the rules stated that if a passenger wanted the train then the train had to stop. The driver applied the brakes and the train came to a halt. He leaned out of the cab and shouted back along the platform to McMurdo, 'Where are you going this time of night, Davie?'

'Oh, I'm not getting on,' said Davie McMurdo. 'I just wanted to tell you my wife will be getting on in the morning!'

THE JOURNEY THAT NEVER WAS

ENGLAND, 1936

Prejudice against the railway lasted well into the twentieth century. In a few remote parts of Britain men and women who'd been young when the railway first came to their districts in the 1860s and 1870s grew up with a loathing for the new method of transport that no amount of familiarity would dispel.

One elderly Westmorland farmer travelled once on the train when he was in his twenties and was terrified by the experience: 'I knew immediately this noise and chaos and terror meant no good to the future of mankind!' He is reported to have vowed not only never to travel again by train but also to forbid any member of his family ever to travel by train.

The old man had no children, but late in his long life (when he was in his eighties, in fact) he developed a fondness for a great-nephew who was in his early teens. He told the young man's parents that he would make the boy his heir – and he had amassed a significant fortune – but only on condition that the young man sign a legal contract agreeing that he would never travel on 'that ungodly iron road that has been the curse of our age'.

Despite the bizarre nature of the request the young man and his parents agreed that for the sake of the legacy he should sign, which he duly did in 1936, in front of the old man, a lawyer and several witnesses. And he was as good as his word – by all accounts he simply moved into the old man's farmhouse when the old man finally died and he kept his promise. He died in the 1960s having never, so far as anyone could tell, travelled by train. An example perhaps of the most extraordinary train journey that never happened!

BEECHAM'S HOWLERS

ENGLAND, 1938

The great conductor and eccentric Sir Thomas Beecham was travelling in a non-smoking compartment on a train belonging to the Great Western Railway. A lady entered the compartment and lit a cigarette, saying, 'I'm sure you won't object if I smoke.'

'Not at all,' replied Beecham, 'provided that you don't object if I'm sick.'

'I don't think you know who I am,' the lady haughtily pointed out. 'I'm one of the directors' wives.'

'Madam,' said Beecham, 'if you were the director's only wife I should still be sick.'

CAKE SHOP

ENGLAND, 1955

With its hundreds of miles of tunnels, the London Underground has always been the focus of strange and sometimes bizarre tales. One of the spookiest happened in the winter of 1955.

Jack Hayden had worked as a ticket collector at Covent Garden station for many years without incident. Then late one November night, just as he was preparing to close the station after the last train had been through, he came across a man wearing a top hat and tails at the top of the stairs. He said later that there had been something very odd about this chap – he smiled but did not speak and vanished into the night when Hayden unlocked the gate and let him out.

A week or so later, Hayden saw the same man dressed exactly as before, but when he spoke to him he turned and walked quickly away. By the time Hayden had caught up with him the man had turned a corner and vanished.

Soon the station was buzzing with rumours about who this mysterious man might be – other railwaymen caught glimpses of him and the story eventually reached the newspapers. Hayden was interviewed and asked to work with an artist to produce a likeness of the mystery man.

After the identikit picture had been published several people immediately recognised the extraordinary similarity between the drawing of the mystery man and the long-dead actor William Terriss (1847–97).

Terriss has been seen on several occasions since 1955, and though it was long thought that his restless spirit perhaps harboured a grievance against the land of the living, the more likely explanation for his occasional appearances was that Covent Garden station was built on the site of Terriss's favourite cake shop.

MAGGOT BOX

ENGLAND, 1965

He was a little-known author, the last of that now-vanished species of professional hacks who, given a good brief and a reasonable amount of time, could turn out a good workmanlike book on pretty much any subject. The freelance nature of his work also meant he had plenty of time to pursue his favourite sport, which was fishing. To be absolutely precise he liked fishing the Thames, and was often to be found wandering some little-known reach of the river in search of a forgotten backwater or a deep eddy that might contain a 5-pound chub or a 10-pound barbel or even, that most rare thing, a Thames trout.

On this particular day he was travelling to Windsor on the train from Paddington. Usually, he avoided the rush-hour period and set off long before most travellers were even out of bed, but on this particular day he'd overslept and was now sitting in a crowded carriage surrounded by smartly dressed businessmen, mothers with their children, students and tourists.

Our fisherman author didn't carry much with him in the way of tackle but he liked to take plenty of bait and on this occasion he had a truly massive bait box filled to the very brim with some of the biggest, liveliest maggots he'd ever seen. The box must have contained at least two gallons of the little larvae.

The train was hot and crowded. The fisherman was tired. He soon fell fast asleep, and suddenly, without knowing quite where he was, he was woken by deafening shouts and screams. At first he thought the train must have crashed. All along the carriage men, women and children were jumping about and uttering loud cries of disgust and fear. The fisherman was stunned – or at least he was until he happened to glance down at his tackle bag and bait box. Somehow the bait box had managed to tip over on its side and its lid had come off. Well over half the maggots had spilled on to the carriage floor. While he'd been asleep the motion of the train and the maggots' ceaseless crawling had distributed them evenly over virtually the whole of the carriage from one end to the other.

Thinking he was very likely to be lynched if discovered, our intrepid angler hastily picked up his bits and pieces and made a quick getaway through the connecting door into the next carriage. Having carefully replaced the bait box lid, he settled down for a further nap.

THE LAST OIL LAMPS
ENGLAND, 1998

A traveller on a Somerset line was astonished as his train entered the station at Yeovil Pen Mill to see that the semaphore signals were lit by oil lamps. He thought he must be dreaming, but on making enquiries discovered that every week since the station had opened in 1857 a railwayman had topped up the 24 lamps with paraffin and trimmed their wicks.

The oil lamps had long outlasted the steam era and British Railways simply because, like much of the so-called old technology of the steam era, they were well-designed and did their job efficiently. But in the end, efficiency alone was not enough to save them, and this last link with the early railway gave way at last to twentieth-century technology.

MYSTERY MONEY

ENGLAND, 2003

A schoolboy travelling from Reading to Paddington found a small attaché case filled with £20 notes. There was nothing especially odd about that, perhaps as the area around Reading is home to many wealthy individuals, and the line into Paddington is always packed with businessmen and civil servants heading into London each day.

But what made this particular find so odd was the writing pad found in the same case. The schoolboy had no idea what language was written in the notepad, and when he took the case to the local police they were equally baffled.

Experts from Reading University were called in and they too were stumped until a professor of Ancient Greek mentioned the notes he'd seen to an archaeologist friend. He described the few letters he could remember from his examination of the notebook, and the archaeologist correctly identified the script as cuneiform (a wedge-shaped system of writing invented by the Sumerians, a society that first developed in what is now southern Iraq in around 4000BC). When the notes were examined again the identification was confirmed, but even for scholars who understood the form of writing known as Ugaritic, the text made no sense. It used Ugaritic cuneiform script but in what looked like random sequences.

Ugaritic was only discovered in 1929 on tablets uncovered by accident on the site of the ruined city of Ugarit, modern-day Ras Shamra, in what is now Syria. The tablets were deciphered in 1930. Ugaritic is an ancient Semitic language (similar to Arabic) used from the fourteenth to the twelfth century BC and known only from this one site. But why anyone should have written out random examples of this ancient language and then placed them in a case with £2,000 has never been explained.

The police kept the money for six months in case its rightful owner should appear, but no one ever came forward and the money was returned to the boy. This strange mystery remains unsolved.

VANISHING VIOLIN
ENGLAND, 2007

Musician Karen Warren was travelling from Edinburgh to Peterborough with her extremely valuable eighteenth-century violin. She took a call on her mobile phone and walked a short distance along the carriage from her seat. When she returned a few moments later her violin had vanished. She ran from one end of the train to the other, frantically asking if any of the passengers had seen someone carrying a violin. The violin had a very distinctive case with the letters 'KW' on it, yet apparently no one had seen a thing.

At Peterborough she reported the theft to the police and began to wonder if her insurance would cover the cost of a replacement. She was panicking, too, as she needed a violin for a concert in two days' time. She telephoned her colleagues in the orchestra and arranged to borrow a violin for the upcoming concert, but it was difficult to practise with all the worry of insurance claims and the real possibility she would never see her beloved instrument again.

So it was with a heavy heart that she arrived at the concert hall and entered the auditorium ready to rehearse. Hardly daring to believe her eyes, she saw her lost violin, in its case and neatly placed on her usual seat in the first violins. The reappearance of the violin was never explained but it had contained her address and perhaps the thief had regretted his action and decided to return the violin – but how on earth did he know where she was next due to play?

PLUM JOB
ENGLAND, 2008

The old joke about trains being delayed because of leaves on the line is no joke at all if you work on the railways. The problem is that modern diesel and electric locomotives are not heavy enough to crush through wet autumn leaves so their wheels spin helplessly in the mush, especially when the train is trying to climb a gradient.

Old steam engines, on the other hand, were so heavy they made light work of wet leaves. The whole problem of slippery rails received a new twist in 2008, when a local newspaper reported that trains to London from Brighton were delayed, not because of wet leaves on the line but, of all things, too many plums.

The problem occurred on an incline north of Brighton where wild plum trees had colonised the embankment. When the fruit fell late in the year, followed by the rain, the tracks turned into a sticky, slushy mush that prevented train wheels getting any traction. The result: late and delayed trains. Having been mercilessly teased about leaves on the line, train officials decided not to put out an official explanation blaming plums!

ACKNOWLEDGEMENTS

A number of people helped point me in the direction of dusty archives, rare books and long-vanished newspapers and magazines – without their assistance some of the best stories in this book would not have seen the light of day. Bill Wycherley let me dig through his collection of railway ephemera; Richard Westall allowed me to take over his attic for a week; Alf Lloyd sent me some hilarious stories based on personal memories and Jo Davis of the Wimbledon Wheeltappers and Shunters Historical Society got me out of a sticky corner on several occasions.